The Historic Elm at Cambridge, Massachusetts, Where Washington Took Command of the American Army, July 3, 1775. (*From a photograph made some years before it fell on October 28, 1923*)

# AMERICA

## Great Crises In Our History
## Told by Its Makers

### A LIBRARY OF ORIGINAL SOURCES

Volume III
Revolution
1753—1783

ISSUED BY

## AMERICANIZATION DEPARTMENT

## VETERANS OF FOREIGN WARS
#### OF THE
## UNITED STATES

CHICAGO, U. S. A.

# TABLE OF CONTENTS

## VOLUME III

5

# TABLE OF CONTENTS

# 8 TABLE OF CONTENTS

# REVOLUTION
## 1753—1783

# WASHINGTON'S EXPEDITION TO THE OHIO

*From Washington's Journal*

*THE French and English were both claiming the Ohio country. In Virginia the Ohio Company was organized to settle and develop the new territory. About the same time the French began occupying it and erecting forts to safeguard their possessions. The Virginia Company decided to send a messenger to the French to order them out.*

*Their first messenger was an experienced frontiersman who lost courage and came home. It was then that Governor Dinwiddy decided to send George Washington on the perilous expedition. That he should have been selected for this hazardous journey when only 21 years of age is a lasting tribute to the high character of the youthful Washington.*

*Washington kept a journal of his expedition and Governor Dinwiddy was so favorably impressed with it that he decided to have it published at once, and gave Washington only 24 hours to put it in the hands of the printer, William Hunter, who published it at Williamsburg in January, 1754.*

I WAS commissioned and appointed by the Honorable Robert Dinwiddy, Esq; Governor, &c., of Virginia, to visit and deliver a letter to the Commandant of the French forces on the Ohio, and set out on the intended journey the same day: The next, I arrived at Fredericksburg, and engaged Mr. Jacob Vanbraam (formerly Washington's fencing-master) to be my French interpreter; and proceeded with him to Alexandria, where we provided necessaries. From thence we went to Winchester, and got baggage, horses, &c.; 'and from thence we pursued the new road to Wills-Creek (now Cumberland, Md.) where we arrived the 14th of November.

Here I engaged Mr. Gist to pilot us out, and also hired four others as servitors, Barnaby Currin and John Mac-Quire, Indian traders, Henry Steward, and William Jenkins; and in company with those persons, left the inhabitants the day following.

The excessive rains and vast quantity of snow which had fallen, prevented our reaching Mr. Frazier's, an Indian trader, at the mouth of Turtle Creek, on Monongahela [river], till Thursday, the 22d. We were informed here, that expresses had been sent a few days before to the traders down the river, to acquaint them with the French General's death, and the return of the major part of the French army into winter quarters.

The waters were quite impassable, without swimming our horses; which obliged us to get the loan of a canoe from Frazier, and to send Barnaby Currin and Henry Steward down the Monongahela, with our baggage, to meet us at the forks of Ohio, about 10 miles, there to cross the Aligany.

As I got down before the canoe, I spent some time in viewing the rivers, and the land in the fork; which I think extremely well situated for a fort, as it has the absolute command of both rivers. The land at the point is 20 or 25 feet above the common surface of the water; and a considerable bottom of flat, well-timbered land all around it, very convenient for building: The rivers are each a quarter of a mile, or more, across, and run here very near at right angles: Aligany bearing N. E. and Monongahela S. E. The former of these two is a very rapid and swift running water; the other deep and still, without any perceptible fall.

About two miles from this, on the south east side of the river, at the place where the Ohio Company intended to erect a fort, lives Shingiss, king of the Delawares: We called upon him, to invite him to council at the Loggs-town.

As I had taken a good deal of notice yesterday of the situation at the forks, my curiosity led me to examine this more particularly, and I think it greatly inferior, either for defense or advantages; especially the latter: For a fort at the forks would be equally well situated on the Ohio, and have the entire command of the Monongahela: which runs up to our settlements and is extremely well designed for water carriage, as it is of a deep still nature. Besides a fort at the fork might be built at a much less expense, than at the other place.

Nature has well contrived this lower place, for water defense; but the hill whereon it must stand being about a quarter of a mile in length, and then descending gradually on the land side, will render it difficult and very expensive, to make a sufficient fortification there.—The whole flat upon the hill must be taken-in, the side next the descent made extremely high, or else the hill itself cut away: Otherwise, the enemy may raise batteries within that distance without being exposed to a single shot from the fort.

Shingiss attended us to the Loggs-Town, where we arrived between sun-setting and dark, the 25th day after I left Williamsburg. We traveled over some extreme good and bad land, to get to this place.—

As soon as I came into town, I went to Mona-katoocha (as the half-king was out at his hunting-cabin on little Beaver-Creek, about 15 miles off) and informed him by John Davison, my Indian interpreter, that I was sent a messenger to the French General; and was ordered to call upon the Sachems of the Six Nations, to acquaint them with it.—I gave him a string of wampum, and a twist of tobacco, and desired him to send for the half-king; which he promised to do by a runner in the morning, and for other sachems.— I invited him and the other great men present to my tent, where they stayed about an hour and returned.

According to the best observations I could make, Mr. Gist's new settlement (which we passed by) bears about W. N. W. 70 miles from Wills-Creek; Shana-pins, or the forks N. by W. or N. N. W. about 50 miles from that; and from thence to the Loggs-Town, the course is nearly west about 18 or 20 miles: so that the whole distance, as we went and computed it, is at least 135 or 140 miles from our back inhabitants.

25th.  Came to town four or ten Frenchmen who had deserted from a company at the Kuskuskas, which lies at the mouth of this river. I got the following account from them. They were sent from New Orleans with 100 men, and 8 canoe-loads of pro-visions to this place; where they expected to have met the same number of men, from the forts on this side Lake Erie, to convey them and the stores up, who were not arrived when they ran-off.

I enquired into the situation of the French, on the Mississippi, their number, and what forts they had built. They informed me, that there were four small forts between New Orleans and the Black-Islands, garrisoned with about 30 or 40 men, and a few small pieces in each. That at New Orleans, which is near the mouth of the Mississippi, there are 35 companies, of 40 men each, with a pretty strong fort mounting 8 carriage guns; and at the Black-Islands there are several companies, and a fort with 6 guns. The Black-Islands are about 130 leagues above the mouth of the Ohio, which is about 350 above New Orleans. They also acquainted me that there was a small palisadoed fort on the Ohio, at the mouth of the Obaish about 60 leagues from the Mississippi. The Obaish heads near the west end of Lake Erie, and affords the communication between the French on Mississippi and those on the Lakes. These deserters came up from the lower Shanoah Town with one Brown, an Indian Trader, and were going to Philadelphia.

About 3 o'clock this evening the half-king came to town. I went up and invited him with Davison, privately, to my tent; and desired him to relate some of the particulars of his journey to the French Commandant, and reception there: Also to give me an account of the ways and distance. He told me that the nearest and levelest way was now impassable, by reason of many large mirey savannas; that we must be obliged to go by Venango, and should not get to the near fort under 5 or 6 nights sleep, good traveling.  When he went to the fort he said he was received in a very stern manner by the late Commander; who asked him very abruptly, what he had come about, and to declare his business: Which he said he did in the following speech:—

FATHERS, I am come to tell you your own speeches; what your own mouths have declared.  Fathers, you in former days, set a silver basin before us, wherein there was the leg of a beaver, and desired all the nations to come and eat of it; to eat in peace and plenty, and not to be churlish to one another: and that if any such person should be found to be a disturber, I here lay down by the edge of the dish a rod, which you must scourge them with; and if I your father, should get foolish, in my old days, I desire you may use it upon me as well as others.

Now fathers, it is you who are the disturbers in this land, by coming and building your towns; and taking it away unknown to us, and by force.

Fathers, we kindled a fire a long time ago, at a place called Montreal, where we desired you to stay, and not to come and intrude upon our land.  I now desire you may dispatch to that place; for be it known to you, fathers, that this is our land, and not yours.

Fathers, I desire you may hear me in civilness; if not, we must handle that rod which

was laid down for the use of the obstreperous.
If you had come in a peaceable manner, like
our brothers the English, we should not have
been against your trading with us, as they do;
but to come, fathers, and build houses upon
our land, and to take it by force, is what we
cannot submit to.

Fathers, both you and the English are white,
we live in a country between; therefore the
land belongs to neither one nor t'other: But
the great Being above allowed it to be a place
of residence for us; so fathers, I desire you to
withdraw, as I have done our brothers the
English; for I will keep you at arm's length.
I lay this down as a trial for both, to see which
will have the greatest regard to it, and that
side we will stand by and make equal shares
with us. Our brothers, the English, have
heard this, and I come now to tell it to you; for
I am not afraid to discharge you off this land.

This he said was the substance of what he spoke
to the General, who made this reply:

"Now my child, I have heard your speech:
you spoke first, but it is my time to speak
now. Where is my wampum that you took
away, with the marks of towns in it? This
wampum I do not know, which you have discharged me off the land with; but you need
not put yourself to the trouble of speaking, for
I will not hear you. I am not afraid of flies,
or mosquitos, for Indians are such as those.
I tell you, down that river I will go, and will
build upon it, according to my command. If

the river was blocked up, I have forces sufficient to burst it open and tread under my feet
all that stand in opposition, together with their
alliances; for my force is as the sand upon the
sea shore: therefore, here is your wampum,
I fling it at you. Child, you talk foolish; you
say this land belongs to you, but there is not
the black of my nail yours. I saw that land
sooner than you did, before the Shannoahs and
you were at war: Lead was the man who
went down and took possession of that river:
It is my land, and I will have it, let who will
stand-up for, or say-against it. I'll buy and
sell with the English (mockingly). If people
will be ruled by me, they may expect kindness,
but not else."

The Half-King told me he inquired of the General
after two Englishmen who were made prisoners, and
received this answer:

"Child, you think it is a very great hardship
that I made prisoners of those two people at
Venango. Don't you concern yourself with
it: We took and carried them to Canada, to
get intelligence of what the English were
doing in Virginia."

He informed me that they had built two forts, one
on Lake Erie (Fort Presque Isle, within the present
limits of Erie), and another on French-Creek (Fort
le Bœuf. It stood near the present town of Water-
ford, Pa.) near a small lake about 15 miles asunder,
and a large wagon road between: They are both built

after the same model, but different in the size; that on the lake the largest. He gave me a plan of them, of his own drawing.

The Indians inquired very particularly after their brothers in Carolina jail.

They also asked what sort of boy it was who was taken from the south-branch; for they were told by some Indians, that a party of French Indians had carried a white boy by the Kuskuska Town, towards the lakes.

26th. We met in council at the Long-House, about 9 o'clock, where I spoke to them as follows:

"Brothers, I have called you together in Council by order of your brother, the Governor of Virginia, to acquaint you, that I am sent, with all possible dispatch, to visit, and deliver a letter to the French Commandant, of very great importance to your brothers, the English; and I dare say, to you their friends and allies.

"I was desired, brothers, by your brother the Governor, to call upon you, the Sachems of the Nations, to inform you of it, and to ask your advice and assistance to proceed the nearest and best road to the French. You see, brothers, I have gotten thus far on my journey.

"His Honor likewise desired me to apply to you for some of your young men, to conduct and provide provisions for us on our way; and be a safeguard against those French Indians who have taken up the hatchet against us. I have spoken this particularly to you brothers, because his Honor our Governor treats you as good friends and allies; and holds you in great esteem.  To confirm what I have said, I give you this string of wampum."

After they had considered for some time on the above discourse, the half-king got up and spoke:—

Now, my brothers, in regard to what my brother the Governor has desired me, I return you this answer.

I rely upon you as a brother ought to do, as you say we are brothers and one people: We shall put heart in hand and speak to our fathers and French concerning the speech they made to me; and you may depend that we will endeavor to be your guard.

Brother, as you have asked my advice, I hope you will be ruled by it and stay till I can provide a company to go with you.  The French speech-belt is not here.  I have it to go for to my hunting cabin: Likewise the people whom I have ordered in, are not yet come, nor cannot till the third night from this: till which time, brother, I must beg you to stay.

I intend to send a guard of Mingo's Shannoah's and Delawares, that our brothers may see the love and loyalty we bear them.

As I had orders to make all possible dispatch, and waiting here was very contrary to my inclinations, I thanked him in the most suitable manner I could; and told him, that my business required the greatest expedition, and would not admit of that delay.  He was not well pleased that I should offer to go before the time he had appointed, and told me, that he could not consent to our going without a guard, for fear some accident should befall us and draw a reflection upon him.  Besides, says he, this is a matter of no small moment, and must not be entered into without due consideration:  For now I intend to deliver up the French speech-belt, and make the Shannoahs and Delawares do the same.  And accordingly he gave orders to King Shingiss, who was present, to attend on Wednesday night with the wampum; and two men of their nation to be in readiness to set-out with us next morning.  As I found it was impossible to get-off without affronting them in the most egregious manner, I consented to stay.

I gave them back a string of wampum which I met with at Mr. Frazier's, and which they had sent with a speech to his Honor the Governor, to inform him, that three nations of French Indians, viz: Chippoways, Ottoways, and Orundaks had taken-up the hatchet against the English; and desired them to repeat it over again:  But this they postponed doing till they met in full council with the Shannoahs and Delaware chiefs.

27th.  Runners were now dispatched very early for the Shannoah chiefs.  The half-king set out himself to fetch the French speech-belt from his hunting cabin.

28th.  He returned this evening, and came with Monokatoocha, and two other Sachems to my tent, and begged (as they had complied with his Honor the Governor's request, in providing men, &c.) to know on what business we were going to the French? this was a question I all along expected, and had provided as satisfactory answers to, as I could; which allayed their curiosity a little.

Monokatoocha informed me, that an Indian from Venango brought news, a few days ago, that the French had called all the Mingo's, Delawares, &c., together at that place; and told them, that they intended to have been down the river this fall, but the waters were growing cold, and the winter advancing, which obliged them to go into quarters: But that they might assuredly expect them in the spring, with a far greater number; and desired that they might be quite passive, and not to intermeddle, unless they had a mind to draw all their force upon them: For that they expected to fight the English three years (as they supposed there would be some attempts made to stop them), in which time they should conquer: But that if they should prove equally strong, they and the English would join to cut them all off, and divide the land between them: That though they had lost their general, and some few of their soldiers, yet there were men enough to reinforce them, and make them masters of the Ohio.

This speech, he said, was delivered to them by one Captain Joncaire, their interpreter in chief, living at Venango, and a man of note in the army.

29th. The half-king and Monokatoocha came very early, and begged me to stay one day more: For notwithstanding they had used all the diligence in their power, the Shannoah chiefs had not brought the wampum they ordered, but would certainly be in to-night; if not, they would delay me no longer, but would send it after us as soon as they arrived.— When I found them so pressing in their request, and knew that returning of wampum was the abolishing of agreements; and giving this up, was shaking-off all dependence upon the French, I consented to stay, as I believed an offense offered at this crisis, might be attended with greater ill consequence, than another day's delay. They also informed me, that Shingiss could not get in his men; and was prevented from coming himself by his wife's sickness (I believe, by fear of the French); but that the wampum of that nation was lodged with Kustaloga one of their chiefs at Venango.

In the evening late they came again and acquainted me that the Shannoahs were not yet arrived, but that it should not retard the prosecution of our journey. He delivered in my hearing, the speeches that were to be made to the French by Jeskakake, one of their old chiefs, which was giving up the belt the late Commandant had asked for, and repeating near the same speech he himself had done before.

He also delivered a string of wampum to this chief, which was sent by King Shingiss, to be given to Kustaloga, with orders to repair to the French, and deliver up the wampum.

He likewise gave a very large string of black and white wampum, which was to be sent up immediately to the six nations, if the French refused to quit the land at this warning; which was the third and last time, and was the right of this Jeskakake to deliver.

30th.  Last night the great men assembled to their council-house, to consult further about this journey, and who were to go:  The result of which was, that only three of their chiefs, with one of their best hunters, should be our convoy.  The reason they gave for not sending more, after what had been proposed at council the 26th, was, that a greater number might give the French suspicions of some bad design, and cause them to be treated rudely:  But I rather think they could not get their hunters in.

We set out about 9 o'clock with the half-king Jeskakake, White Thunder, and the Hunter; and traveled on the road to Venango, where we arrived the 4th of December, without any thing remarkable happening but a continued series of bad weather.

This is an old Indian town, situated at the mouth of French Creek on Ohio: and lies near N. about 60 miles from the Loggs-Town, but more than 70 the way we were obliged to go.

We found the French colors hoisted at a house from which they had driven Mr. John Frasier, an English subject.  I immediately repaired to it, to know where the Commander resided.  There were three officers, one of whom, Capt. Joncaire, informed me, that he had the command of the Ohio: But that there was a general officer at the near fort, where he advised me to apply for an answer. He invited us to sup with them; and treated us with the greatest complaisance.

The wine, as they dosed themselves pretty plentifully with it, soon banished the restraint which at first appeared in their conversation; and gave a license to their tongues to reveal their sentiments more freely.

They told me, that it was their absolute design to take possession of the Ohio, and by G—— they would do it: For that although they were sensible the English could raise two men for their one; yet they knew their motions were too slow and dilatory to prevent any undertaking of theirs. They pretend to have an undoubted right to the river, from a discovery made by one La Salle 60 years ago; and the rise of this expedition is, to prevent our settling on the river or waters of it, as they had heard of some families moving out in order thereto. From the best intelligence I could get, there have been 1,500 men on their side Ontario Lake: But upon the death of the general all were recalled to about 6 or 700, who were left to garrison four forts, 150 or there abouts in each. The first of them is on French Creek near a small lake, about 60 miles from Venango, near N. N. W. the next lies on Lake Erie, where the greater part of their stores are kept, about 15 miles from the other. From this it is 120 miles to the carrying place at the falls of Lake Erie where there is a small fort; which they lodge their goods at, in bringing them from Montreal, the place whence all their stores come from. The next fort lies about 20 miles from this, on Ontario Lake. Between this fort and Montreal there are three others, the first of which is near opposite to the English Fort Oswego. From the fort on Lake Erie to Montreal is about 600 miles, which they say requires no more, if good weather, than four weeks' voyage, if they go in barks or large vessels, so that they may cross the lake: But if they come in canoes it will require 5 or 6 weeks, for they are obliged to keep under the shore.

5th. Rained excessively all day, which prevented our traveling. Capt. Joncaire sent for the half-king, as he had but just heard that he came with me: He affected to be much concerned that I did not make free to bring them in before. I excused it in the best manner I was capable, and told him, I did not think their company agreeable, as I had heard him say a good deal in dispraise of Indians in general. But another motive prevented me from bringing them into his company: I knew he was interpreter, and a person of very great influence among the Indians, and had lately used all possible means to draw them over to their interest; therefore I was desirous of giving no opportunity that could be avoided.

When they came in, there was great pleasure expressed at seeing them. He wondered how they could be so near without coming to visit him; made several trifling presents; and applied liquor so fast, that they were soon rendered incapable of the business they came about, notwithstanding the caution which was given.

6th. The half-king came to my tent, quite sober, and insisted very much that I should stay and hear what he had to say to the French. I fain would have prevented his speaking anything till he came to the Commandant, but could not prevail. He told me that at this place a council fire was kindled, where all their business with these people was to be transacted; and that the management of the Indian affairs was left solely to Monsieur Joncaire. As I was desirous of knowing the issue of this, I agreed to stay, but sent our horses a little way up French Creek to raft over and encamp; which I knew would make it near night.

About 10 o'clock they met in council. The King spoke much the same as he had before done to the General, and offered the French speech-belt which had before been demanded, with the marks of four towns on it, which Monsieur Joncaire refused to receive; but desired him to carry it to the fort to the Commander.

7th. Monsieur La Force, commissary of the French stores, and three other soldiers came over to accompany us up. We found it extremely difficult to get the Indians off to-day, as every stratagem had been used to prevent their going-up with me. I had last night, left John Davison (the Indian interpreter whom I brought with me from town), and strictly charged him not to be out of their company, as I could not get them over to my tent; for they had some business with Kustaloga, and chiefly to know the reason why he did not deliver up the French belt which he had in keeping: But I was obliged to send Mr. Gist over to-day to fetch them; which he did with great persuasion.

At 11 o'clock we set out for the fort, and were prevented from arriving there till the 11th by excessive rains, snows, and bad traveling, through many mires and swamps. These we were obliged to pass, to avoid crossing the creek, which was impossible, either by fording or rafting, the water was so high and rapid.

We passed over much good land since we left Venango, and through several extensive and very rich meadows; one of which I believe was near four miles in length, and considerably wide in some places.

12th. I prepared early to wait upon the Commander, and was received and conducted to him by the second officer in command. I acquainted him with my business, and offered my commission and letter, both of which he desired me to keep till the arrival of Monsieur Riparti, Captain at the next fort, who was sent for and expected every hour.

This Commander is a knight of the military order of St. Lewis, and named Legardeur de St. Pierre. He is an elderly gentleman, and has much the air of a soldier. He was sent over to take the command immediately upon the death of the late General, and arrived here about seven days before me.

At 2 o'clock the gentleman who was sent for arrived, when I offered the letter, &c, again; which they received, and adjourned into a private apartment for the captain to translate, who understood a little English. After he had done it, the Commander desired I would walk in, and bring my interpreter to peruse and correct it; which I did.

13th. The chief officers retired, to hold a council of war; which gave me an opportunity of taking the dimensions of the fort, and making what observations I could.

It is situated on the south or west fork of French Creek, near the water; and is almost surrounded by the creek, and a small branch of it which forms a kind of island. Four houses compose the sides. The bastions are made of piles driven into the ground, standing more than 12 feet above it, and sharp at top: With port-holes cut for cannon, and loop-holes for the small arms to fire through. There are eight 6 lb. pieces mounted, in each bastion; and one piece of four pound before the gate. In the bastions are a guard-house, chapel, doctor's lodging, and the Commander's private store, around which are laid platforms for the cannon and men to stand on. There are several barracks without the fort, for the soldiers' dwelling; covered, some with bark and some with boards, made chiefly of logs. There are also several other houses, such as stables, smiths shop, &c.

I could get no certain account of the number of men here: But according to the best judgment I could form, there are an hundred exclusive of officers, of which there are many. I also gave orders to the people who were with me, to take an exact account of the canoes which were hauled-up to convey their forces down in the spring. This they did, and told 50 of birch bark, and 170 of pine; besides many others which were blocked-out, in readiness to make.

14th. As the snow increased very fast, and our horses daily became weaker, I sent them off unloaded; under the care of Barnaby Currin, and two others, to make all convenient dispatch to Venango, and there wait our arrival, if there was a prospect of the rivers freezing, if not, then to continue down to Shanapin's Town, at the forks of Ohio, and there to wait till we came to cross Aliganey; intending myself to go down by water, as I had the offer of a canoe or two.

As I found many plots concerted to retard the Indians' business, and prevent their returning with me; I endeavored all that lay in my power to frustrate their schemes, and hurry them on to execute their intended design. They accordingly pressed for admittance this evening, which at length was granted them, privately, with the Commander and one or two other officers. The half-king told me, that he offered the wampum to the Commander, who evaded taking it, and made many fair promises of love and friendship; said he wanted to live in peace, and trade amicably with them, as a proof of which he would send some goods immediately down to the Loggs-Town for them. But I rather think the design of that is, to bring away all our straggling traders they meet with, as I privately understood they intended to carry an officer, &c, with them. And what rather confirms this opinion, I was inquiring of the Commander, by what authority he had made prisoners of several of our English subjects. He told me that the country belonged to them; that no Englishman had a right to trade upon those waters; and that he had orders to make every person prisoner who attempted it on the Ohio, or the waters of it.

I inquired of Capt. Riparti about the boy who was carried by this place, as it was done while the command devolved on him, between the death of the late General, and the arrival of the present. He acknowledged, that a boy had been carried past; and that the Indians had two or three white men's scalps (I was told by some of the Indians at Venango eight) but pretended to have forgotten the name of the place which the boy came from, and all the particular facts, though he had questioned him for some hours, as they were carrying him past. I likewise inquired what they had done with John Trotter and James Mac-Clocklan, two Pennsylvania traders, whom they had taken, with all their goods. They told me, that they had been sent to Canada, but were now returned home.

This evening I received an answer to his Honor the Governor's letter from the Commandant.

15th. The Commandant ordered a plentiful store of liquor, provision, &c, to be put on board our canoe; and appeared to be extremely complaisant, though he was exerting every artifice which he could invent to set our own Indians at variance with us, to prevent their going 'till after our departure. Presents, rewards, and everything which could be suggested by him or his officers.—I can't say that ever in my life I suffered so much anxiety as I did in this affair: I saw that every stratagem which the most fruitful brain could invent, was practiced, to win the half-king to their interest; and that leaving him here was giving them the opportunity they aimed at.—I went to the half-king and pressed him in the strongest terms to go: He told me the Commandant would not discharge him till the morning. I then went to the Commandant, and desired him to do their business; and complained of ill treatment: For keeping them, as they were part of my company, was detaining me. This he promised not to do, but to forward my journey as much as he could. He protested he did not keep them, but was ignorant of the cause of their stay; though I soon found it out:—He had promised them a present of guns, &c, if they would wait 'till the morning.

As I was very much pressed, by the Indians, to wait this day for them, I consented, on a promise, that nothing should hinder them in the morning.

16th. The French were not slack in their inventions to keep the Indians this day also: But as they were obligated, according to promise, to give the present, they then endeavored to try the power of liquor; which I doubt not would have prevailed at any other time than this. But I urged and insisted with the King so closely upon his word, that he refrained, and set off with us as he had engaged.

We had a tedious and very fatiguing passage down the creek. Several times we had like to have been staved against rocks; and many times were obliged all hands to get out and remain in the water half an hour or more, getting over the shoals. At one place the ice had lodged and made it impassable by water; therefore we were obliged to carry our canoe across a neck of land, a quarter of a mile over. We did not reach Venango, till the 22d, where we met with our horses.

This creek is extremely crooked, I dare say the distance between the fort and Venango can't be less than 130 miles, to follow the meanders.

23d. When I got things ready to set off, I sent for the half-king, to know whether he intended to go with us, or by water. He told me that White Thunder had hurt himself much, and was sick and unable to walk; therefore he was obliged to carry him down in a canoe. As I found he intended to stay here a day or two, and knew that Monsieur Joncaire would employ every scheme to set him against the English as he had before done; I told him I hoped he would guard against his flattery, and let no fine speeches influence him in their favor. He desired I might not be concerned, for he knew the French too well, for anything to engage him in their behalf; and that though he could not go down with us, he yet would endeavor to meet at the forks with Joseph Campbell, to deliver a speech for me to carry to his Honor the Governor.

He told me he would order the young hunter to attend us, and get provision, &c. if wanted.

Our horses were now so weak and feeble, and the baggage so heavy (as we were obliged to provide all the necessaries which the journey would require) that we doubted much their performing it; therefore myself and others (except the drivers, who were obliged to ride) gave up our horses for packs, to assist along with the baggage. I put myself in an Indian walking dress, and continued with them three days, till I found there was no probability of their getting home in any reasonable time. The horses grew less able to travel every day; the cold increased very fast; and the roads were becoming much worse by a deep snow, continually freezing: Therefore as I was uneasy to get back, to make report of my proceedings to his Honor, the Governor, I determined to prosecute my journey the nearest way through the woods, on foot.

Accordingly I left Mr. Vanbraam in charge of our baggage: with money and directions to provide necessaries from place to place for themselves and horses, and to make the most convenient dispatch in traveling.

I took my necessary papers; pulled off my clothes; and tied myself up in a match coat. Then with gun in hand and pack at my back, in which were my papers and provisions, I set out with Mr. Gist, fitted in the same manner, on Wednesday the 26th.

The day following, just after we had passed a place called the Murdering-Town (where we intended to quit the path, and steer across the country for Shannapins Town) we fell in with a party of French Indians, who had lain in wait for us. One of them fired at Mr. Gist or me, not 15 steps off, but fortunately missed. We took this fellow into custody, and kept him till about 9 o'clock at night; Then let him go, and walked all the remaining part of the night without making any stop; that we might get the start, so far, as to be out of the reach of their pursuit the next day, since we were well assured they would follow our tract as soon as it was light. The next day we continued traveling till quite dark, and got to the river about two miles above Shannapins. We expected to have found the river frozen, but it was not, only about 50 yards from each shore; The ice I suppose had broken up above, for it was driving in vast quantities.

There was no way for getting over but on a raft; Which we set about with but one poor hatchet, and finished just after sun-setting. This was a whole day's work. Then set off; But before we were half way over, we were jammed in the ice, in such a manner that we expected every moment our raft to sink, and ourselves to perish. I put out my setting pole to try to stop the raft, that the ice might pass by; when the rapidity of the stream threw it with so much violence against the pole, that it jerked me out into ten feet of water: but I fortunately saved myself by catching hold of one of the raft logs. Notwithstanding all our efforts we could not get the raft to either shore; but were obliged, as we were near an island, to quit our raft and make to it.

The cold was so extremely severe, that Mr. Gist had all his fingers, and some of his toes frozen; but the water was shut up so hard, that we found no difficulty in getting off the island, on the ice, in the morning, and went to Mr. Frazier's. We met here with 20 warriors who were going to the southward to war, but coming to a place upon the head of the great Kunnaway, where they found seven people killed and scalped (all but one woman with very light hair) they turned about and ran back for fear the inhabitants should rise and take them as the authors of the murder. They report that the bodies were lying about the house, and some of them much torn and eaten by hogs. By the marks which were left, they say they were French Indians of the Ottaway nation, &c., who did it.

As we intended to take horses here, and it required some time to find them, I went-up about three miles to the mouth of Yaughyaughane to visit Queen Aliquippa, who had expressed great concern that we passed her in going to the fort. I made her a present of a matchcoat and a bottle of rum; which latter was thought much the best present of the two.

Tuesday the 1st Day of January, we left Mr. Frazier's house, and arrived at Mr. Gist's at Monongahela the 2d, where I bought a horse, saddle, etc: the 6th we met 17 horses loaded with materials and stores, for a fort at the forks of Ohio, and the day after some families going out to settle: This day we arrived at Wills Creek, after as fatiguing a journey as it is possible to conceive, rendered so by excessive bad weather. From the first day of December to the 15th, there was but one day on which it did not rain or snow incessantly: and throughout the whole journey we met with nothing but one continued series of cold wet weather, which occasioned very uncomfortable lodgings: especially after we had quitted our tent, which was some screen from the inclemency of it.

On the 11th I got to Belvoir: where I stopped one day to take necessary rest; and then set out and arrived in Williamsburgh the 16th; when I waited upon his Honor the Governor with the letter I had brought from the French Commandant; and to give an account of the success of my proceedings. This I beg leave to do by offering the foregoing narrative as it contains the most remarkable occurrences which happened in my journey.

I hope what has been said will be sufficient to make your Honor satisfied with my conduct; for that was my aim in undertaking the journey, and chief study throughout the prosecution of it.

# BENJAMIN FRANKLIN'S PLAN OF UNION

*From Franklin's Original Writings*

*ALTHOUGH the Plan of Union adopted by the Albany Convention, representing seven of the colonies, in 1754, failed, it was the most important federal measure in the colonies before the Revolution. It did not entirely satisfy Franklin himself. "It is not altogether to my mind," he said afterwards, "but it is [as good] as I could get it." And curiously it proved acceptable in almost no quarter, being rejected by the Colonial Assemblies, because, as Franklin records, "there was too much prerogative in it," and rejected by the Board of Trade in England because "it was thought to have too much of the democratic."*

*But the plan familiarized the colonists with the union idea, doing much to prepare them for the Revolutionary struggle twenty years later; and it constitutes a notable landmark in the development of the national principle.*

IT IS proposed, that humble application be made for an act of Parliament of Great Britain, by virtue of which one general government may be formed in America, including all the said colonies, within and under which government each colony may retain its present constitution, except in the particulars wherein a change may be directed by the said act, as hereafter follows.

## PRESIDENT-GENERAL AND GRAND COUNCIL

"That the said general government be administered by a President-General, to be appointed and supported by the crown; and a Grand Council, to be chosen by the representatives of the people of the several Colonies met in their respective assemblies."

It was thought that it would be best the President-General should be supported as well as appointed by the crown, that so all disputes between him and the Grand Council concerning his salary might be prevented; as such disputes have been frequently of mischievous consequence in particular colonies, especially in time of public danger. The quit-rents of crown lands in America might in a short time be sufficient for this purpose. The choice of members for the Grand Council is placed in the House of Representatives of each government, in order to give the people a share in this new general government, as the crown has its share by the appointment of the President-General.

But it being proposed by the gentlemen of the Council of New York, and some other counsellors among the commissioners, to alter the plan in this particular, and to give the governors and councils of the several provinces a share in the choice of the Grand Council, or at least a power of approving and confirming, or of disallowing, the choice made by the House of Representatives, it was said

"That the government or constitution, proposed to be formed by the plan, consists of two branches; a President-General appointed by the crown, and a council chosen by the people, or by the people's representatives, which is the same thing.

"That, by a subsequent article, the council chosen by the people can effect nothing without the consent of the President-General appointed by the crown;

the crown possesses, therefore, full one-half of the power of this constitution.

"That in the British constitution, the crown is supposed to possess but one-third, the lords having their share.

"That this constitution seemed rather more favorable for the crown.

"That it is essential to English liberty, that the subject should not be taxed but by his own consent, or the consent of his elected representatives.

"That taxes to be laid and levied by this proposed constitution will be proposed and agreed to by the representatives of the people, if the plan in this particular be preserved;

"But if the proposed alteration should take place, it seemed as if matters may be so managed, as that the crown shall finally have the appointment, not only of the President-General, but of a majority of the Grand Council; for seven out of eleven governors and councils are appointed by the crown;

"And so the people in all the colonies would in effect be taxed by their governors.

"It was therefore apprehended, that such alterations of the plan would give great dissatisfaction, and that the colonies could not be easy under such a power in governors, and such an infringement of what they take to be English liberty.

"Besides, the giving a share in the choice of the Grand Council would not be equal with respect to all the colonies, as their constitutions differ.  In some,

both governor and council are appointed by the
crown; in others, they are both appointed by the pro-
prietors. In some, the people have a share in the
choice of the council; in others, both government and
council are wholly chosen by the people. But the
House of Representatives is everywhere chosen by
the people; and, therefore, placing the right of choos-
ing the Grand Council in the representatives is equal
with respect to all.

"That the Grand Council is intended to represent
all the several Houses of Representatives of the colonies, as a House of Representatives doth the several
towns or counties of a colony. Could all the people
of a colony be consulted and unite in public measures,
a House of Representatives would be needless, and
could all the assemblies conveniently consult and
unite in general measures, the Grand Council would
be unnecessary.

"That a House of Commons or the House of Representatives, and the Grand Council, are thus alike in
their nature and intention. And, as it would seem
improper that the King or House of Lords should have
a power of disallowing or appointing members of the
House of Commons; so, likewise, that a governor
and council appointed by the crown should have a
power of disallowing or appointing members of the
Grand Council, who, in this constitution, are to be
the representatives of the people.

"If the governors and councils therefore were to
have a share in the choice of any that are to conduct

this general government, it should seem more proper that they choose the President-General. But, this being an office of great trust and importance to the nation, it was thought better to be filled by the immediate appointment of the crown. . . .

### ELECTION OF MEMBERS

"Within—months after the passing such act, the House of Representatives that happen to be sitting within that time, or that shall be especially for that purpose convened, may and shall choose members for the Grand Council, in the following proportion: that is to say, Massachusetts Bay, 7; New Hampshire, 2; Connecticut, 5; Rhode Island, 2; New York, 4; New Jersey, 3; Pennsylvania, 6; Maryland, 4; Virginia, 7; North Carolina, 4; South Carolina, 4.    Total, 48."

It was thought, that if the least colony was allowed two, and the others in proportion, the number would be very great, and the expense heavy; and that less than two would not be convenient, as, a single person being by any accident prevented appearing at the meeting, the colony he ought to appear for would not be represented. That, as the choice was not immediately popular, they would be generally men of good abilities for business, and men of reputation for integrity; and that forty-eight such men might be a number sufficient. But, though it was thought reasonable that each colony should have a share in the representative body in some degree according to the proportion it contributed to the general treasury, yet the proportion of wealth or power of the colonies is not to be judged by the proportion here fixed; because it was at first agreed, that the greatest colony should not have more than seven members, nor the least less than two; and the setting these proportions between these two extremes was not nicely attended to, as it would find itself, after the first election, from the sums brought into the treasury, as by a subsequent article.

### PLACE OF FIRST MEETING

"The Grand Council shall meet for the first time at the city of Philadelphia in Pennsylvania, being called by the President-General as soon as conveniently may be after his appointment."

Philadelphia was named as being nearer the center of the colonies, where the commissioners would be well and cheaply accommodated. The high roads, through the whole extent, are for the most part very good, in which forty or fifty miles a day may very well be, and frequently are, traveled. Great part of the way may likewise be gone by water. In summer time, the passages are frequently performed in a week from Charleston to Philadelphia and New York; and from Rhode Island to New York through the Sound, in two or three days; and from New York to

Philadelphia, by water and land, in two days, by stage, boats, and wheel-carriages that set out every other day. The journey from Charleston to Philadelphia may likewise be facilitated by boats running up Chesapeake Bay three hundred miles. But if the whole journey be performed on horseback, the most distant members, viz., the two from New Hampshire and from South Carolina, may probably render themselves at Philadelphia in fifteen or twenty days; the majority may be there in much less time. . . .

### MEETINGS OF THE GRAND COUNCIL, AND CALL

"The Grand Council shall meet once in every year, and oftener if occasion require, at such time and place as they shall adjourn to at the last preceding meeting, or as they shall be called to meet at by the President-General on any emergency; he having first obtained in writing the consent of seven of the members to such call, and sent due and timely notice to the whole."

It was thought, in establishing and governing new colonies or settlements, regulating Indian trade, Indian treaties, &c., there would every year sufficient business arise to require at least one meeting, and at such meeting many things might be suggested for the benefit of all the colonies. This annual meeting may either be at a time or place certain, to be fixed by the President-General and Grand Council at their first meeting; or left at liberty, to be at such time and place as they shall adjourn to, or be called to meet at by the President-General.

In time of war, it seems convenient that the meeting should be in that colony which is nearest the seat of action.

The power of calling them on any emergency seemed necessary to be vested in the President-General; but, that such power might not be wantonly used to harass the members, and oblige them to make frequent long journeys to little purpose, the consent of seven at least to such call was supposed a convenient guard. . . .

### Members' Allowance

"The members of the Grand Council shall be allowed for their service ten shillings sterling per diem, during their session and journey to and from the place of meeting; twenty miles to be reckoned a day's journey."

It was thought proper to allow some wages, lest the expense might deter some suitable persons from the service; and not to allow too great wages, lest unsuitable persons should be tempted to cabal for the employment, for the sake of gain. Twenty miles were set down as a day's journey, to allow for accidental hindrances on the road, and the greater expenses of traveling than residing at the place of meeting.

### Assent of President-General and His Duty

"The assent of the President-General be requisite to all acts of the Grand Council, and that it be his office and duty to cause them to be carried into execution."

The assent of the President-General to all acts of the Grand Council was made necessary, in order to give the crown its due share of influence in this government, and connect it with that of Great Britain. The President-General, besides one-half of the legislative power, hath in his hands the whole executive power.

### Power of President-General and Grand Council; Treaties of Peace and War

"The President-General, with the advice of the Grand Council, hold or direct all Indian treaties, in which the general interest of the Colonies may be concerned; and make peace or declare war with Indian nations."

The power of making peace or war with Indian nations is at present supposed to be in every colony, and is expressly granted to some by charter, so that no new power is hereby intended to be granted to the colonies. But as, in consequence of this power, one colony might make peace with a nation that another was justly engaged in war with; or make war on slight occasions without the concurrence or approbation of neighboring colonies, greatly endangered by it; or make particular treaties of neutrality in case of a general war, to their own private advantage in trade, by supplying the common enemy; of all which there have been instances; it was thought better to have all treaties of a general nature under a general direction, that so the good of the whole may be consulted and provided for. . . .

### NEW SETTLEMENTS

"They make new settlements on such purchases, by granting lands in the King's name, reserving a quit-rent to the crown for the use of the general treasury."

. . . A particular colony has scarce strength enough to extend itself by new settlements, at so great a distance from the old; but the joint force of the Union might suddenly establish a new colony or two in those parts, or extend an old colony to particular passes, greatly to the security of our present frontiers, increase of trade and people, breaking off the French communication between Canada and Louisiana, and speedy settlement of the intermediate lands.

The power of settling new colonies is therefore thought a valuable part of the plan, and what cannot so well be executed by two unions as by one.

### RAISE SOLDIERS, AND EQUIP VESSELS

"They raise and pay soldiers and build forts for the defense of any of the colonies, and equip vessels of force to guard the coasts and protect the trade on the oceans, lakes, or great rivers; but they shall not impress men in any colony, without the consent of the legislature."

It was thought that quotas of men, to be raised and paid by the several colonies, and joined for any public service, could not always be got together with the necessary expedition. For instance, suppose one thousand men should be wanted in New Hampshire on any emergency. To fetch them by fifties and hundreds out of every colony, as far as South Carolina, would be inconvenient, the transportation chargeable, and the occasion perhaps passed before they could be assembled; and therefore it would be best to raise them (by offering bounty-money and pay) near the place where they would be wanted, to be discharged again when the service should be over.

Particular colonies are at present backward to build forts at their own expense, which they say will be equally useful to their neighboring colonies; who refuse to join, on a presumption that such forts will be built and kept up, though they contribute nothing. This unjust conduct weakens the whole; but the forts being for the good of the whole, it was thought best they should be built and maintained by the whole, out of the common treasury.

In the time of war, small vessels of force are sometimes necessary in the colonies to scour the coasts of small privateers. These being provided by the Union will be an advantage in turn to the colonies which are situated on the sea, and whose frontiers on the land-side, being covered by other colonies, reap but little immediate benefit from the advanced forts.

### Power to Make Laws, Lay Duties, &c.

"For these purposes they have power to make laws, and lay and levy such general duties, imposts, or taxes, as to them shall appear most equal and just (considering the ability and other circumstances of the inhabitants in the several colonies), and such as may be collected with the least inconvenience to the people; rather discouraging luxury, than loading industry with unnecessary burdens."

The laws which the President-General and Grand Council are empowered to make are such only as shall be necessary for the government of the settlements; the raising, regulating, and paying soldiers for the general service; the regulating of Indian trade; and laying and collecting the general duties and taxes. They should also have a power to restrain the exportation of provisions to the enemy from any of the colonies, on particular occasions, in time of war. But it is not intended that they may interfere with the constitution and government of the particular colonies; who are to be left to their own laws, and to lay, levy, and apply their own taxes, as before. . . .

### Each Colony May Defend Itself in Emergency

"The particular military as well as civil establishments in each colony remain in their present state, the general constitution notwithstanding; and that on sudden emergencies any colony may defend itself, and lay the accounts of expense thence arising before the President-General and General Council, who may allow and order payment of the same, as far as they judge such accounts just and reasonable."

Otherwise the union of the whole would weaken the parts, contrary to the design of the union. The accounts are to be judged of by the President-General and the Grand Council, and allowed if found reasonable. This was thought necessary to encourage colonies to defend themselves, as the expense would be light when borne by the whole; and also to check imprudent and lavish expense in such defenses.

# BRADDOCK'S DEFEAT

*Told by his Aide, George Washington*

*IN THIS letter to his mother, Mary, written at Fort Cumberland on July 18, 1755, after the battle in which the English-Colonial forces under General Braddock were defeated and routed by the French and Indians, George Washington describes the historic action in which Braddock was mortally wounded. Everything was abandoned to the enemy—wagons, guns, cattle, horses, baggage and £25,000 in specie, while scores of helpless wounded were left victims of the tomahawk and scalping-knife.*

*Washington, then twenty-three years old, had accompanied Braddock into what is now western Pennsylvania as a volunteer aide-de-camp, and was the only staff officer who escaped uninjured. He read the funeral service over Braddock's grave in the wilderness, while wagons were rolled over the fresh mound lest the General's body be found and desecrated. It still rests there; and until recently no monument, only a clump of trees, marked the grave of this luckless British commander.*

HONORED MADAM: As I doubt not but you have heard of our defeat, and, perhaps, had it represented in a worse light, if possible, than it deserves, I have taken this earliest opportunity to give you some account of the engagement as it happened, within ten miles of the French fort, on Wednesday the 9th instant.

We marched to that place, without any considerable loss, having only now and then a straggler picked up by the French and scouting Indians. When we came there, we were attacked by a party of French and Indians, whose number, I am persuaded, did not exceed three hundred men; while ours consisted of about one thousand three hundred well-armed troops, chiefly regular soldiers, who were struck with such a panic that they behaved with more cowardice than it is possible to conceive. The officers behaved gallantly, in order to encourage their men, for which they suffered greatly, there being near sixty killed and wounded; a large proportion of the number we had.

The Virginia troops showed a good deal of bravery, and were nearly all killed; for I believe, out of three companies that were there, scarcely thirty men are left alive. Captain Peyrouny, and all his officers down to a corporal, were killed. Captain Polson had nearly as hard a fate, for only one of his was left. In short, the dastardly behavior of those they call regulars exposed all others, that were inclined to do their duty, to almost certain death; and, at last, in despite of all the efforts of the officers to the contrary, they ran, as sheep pursued by dogs, and it was impossible to rally them.

The General was wounded, of which he died three days after. Sir Peter Halket was killed in the field, where died many other brave officers. I luckily escaped without a wound, though I had four bullets through my coat, and two horses shot under me. Captains Orme and Morris, two of the aids-de-camp, were wounded early in the engagement, which rendered the duty harder upon me, as I was the only person then left to distribute the General's orders, which I was scarcely able to do, as I was not half recovered from a violent illness, that had confined me to my bed and a wagon for above ten days. I am still in a weak and feeble condition, which induces me to halt here two or three days in the hope of recovering a little strength, to enable me to proceed homewards; from whence, I fear, I shall not be able to stir till toward September; so that I shall not have the pleasure of seeing you till then, unless it be in Fairfax. . . . I am, honored Madam, your most dutiful son.

# THE DEPORTATION OF THE ACADIANS

*By Colonel John Winslow*

ACADIA was originally a French colony which was acquired by the English under the Treaty of Utrecht, and renamed Nova Scotia. In order to destroy the French influence, which continued to predominate, the English Government in 1755 commissioned Colonel Winslow, a Massachusetts officer, to manage the deportation of some 6000 Acadians (probably about half of the total population of French descent) and scatter them among the English colonies to the south. That Winslow, from whose journal, in the Nova Scotia Historical Society, this article is taken, found the task exceedingly disagreeable, indeed painful, is evidenced by his written statement that "The affair is more grievous to me than any service I was ever employed in." The question of the necessity of the removal and dispersion of the Acadians has been much disputed; the historian Parkman thinks it was inevitable. This dramatic event forms the theme of Longfellow's "Evangeline."

LAST evening [August 30, 1755] Captain Murray arrived and brought with him the afore resights commissions and instructions and letters and with whom I consulted methods for removing the whole inhabitants of the villages of Grand Pré, Mines, Rivers Cannard, Habbertong and Gaspereau, and agreed that it would be most convenient to cite all the male inhabitants of said villages to assemble at the church in this place on the 5th of September next to hear the King's orders, and that at the same time Captain Murray to collect the inhabitants of Piziquid, and villages adjacent to Fort Edward for the same purpose, and wrote Colonel Lawrence this day our determination, and after Captain Murray's departure convened the Captains, viz: Adams, Hobbs and Osgood together and after taking an oath of secrecy from them, laid before them my instructions and papers and also of the proposed agreement made between Captain Murray and myself, of which they unanimously approved. . . .

1755, August 31. Sunday. In the afternoon took a tour with Doctor Whitworth and Mr. Gay and 50 men two third parts round Grand Pré. Find abundance of wheat &c on the ground. Returned in the evening. . . .

September 2nd. Set out early in the morning in a whale boat for Fort Edward having with me Doctor Whitworth and adjutant Kennedy to consult with Captain Murray in this critical conjuncture. Confirmed our proposed plan and determined three of the clock in the afternoon to be the time. Made out a citation to the inhabitants to convene them, viz: those in my district at the church in Grand Pré, those of Captain Murray at Fort Edward at Piziquid. Got it put into French by Mr. Beauchamp, a merchant. . . .

September 3rd. This morning Captain Adams and party returned from their march to the River Cannard &c and reported it was a fine country and full of inhabitants, a beautiful church and abundance of the goods of the world. Provisions of all kinds in great plenty. . . .

This day had a consultation with the Captains, the result of which was that I should give out my citation to the inhabitants to-morrow morning. . . .

1755, September the 4th.   This morning sent for Doctor Rodion and delivered him a citation to the inhabitants with a strict charge to see it executed. Which he promised should be faithfully done.

A fine day and the inhabitants very busy about their harvest, &c.

September 5th.   This morning had returns of the horns of the several companies and ordered such as had them to deliver up what cartridges they had to complete those who had no horns, which near about did it and then gave out to those who had horns powder at half a pound each to the amount of half a barrel and twelve balls to each half pound of powder. Ordered the whole camp to lie upon their arms this day.

At three in the afternoon the French inhabitants appeared agreeable to their citation at the church in Grand Pré amounting to 418 of their best men upon which I ordered a table to be set in the center of the church and being attended with those of my officers who were off guard delivered them by interpreters the King's orders in the following words:

Gentlemen,—I have received from his Excellency Governor Lawrence the King's commission which I have in my hand and by whose orders you are convened together to manifest to you his Majesty's final resolution to the French inhabitants of this his province of Nova Scotia.   Who for almost half a century have had more indulgence granted them, than any of his subjects in any part of his dominions.  What use you have made of them you yourself best know.

The part of duty I am now upon is what though necessary, is very disagreeable to my natural make and temper as I know it must be grievous to you who are of the same species.

But it is not my business to animadvert, but to obey such orders as I receive and therefore without hesitation shall deliver you his majesty's orders and instructions, viz:

That your lands and tenements, cattle of all kinds and live stock of all sorts are forfeited to the crown with all other your effects saving your money and household goods and you yourselves to be removed from this his province.

Thus it is peremptorily his Majesty's orders that the whole French inhabitants of these districts, be removed, and I am through his Majesty's goodness directed to allow you liberty to carry of your money and household goods as many as you can without discommoding the vessels you go in.  I shall do everything in my power that all those goods be secured to you and that you are not molested in carrying them off and also that whole families shall go in the same vessel.  And make this remove which I am sensible must give you a great deal of trouble as easy as his Majesty's service will admit and hope that in whatever part of the world you may fall you may be faithful subjects, a peaceable and happy people.

I must also inform you that it is his Majesty's pleasure that you remain in security under the inspection and direction of the troops that I have the honor to command.   And then declared them the King's prisoners. . . .

After delivering these things I returned to my quarters and they the French inhabitants soon moved by their elders that it was a great grief to them, that they had incurred his Majesty's displeasure and that they were fearful that the surprise of their detention here would quite overcome their families whom they had no means to apprise of these their melancholy circumstances and prayed that part of them might be returned as hostages for the appearance of the rest and the bigger number admitted to go home to their families, and that as some of their men were absent they would be obliged to bring them in.   I informed them I would consider of their motion, and report.

And immediately convened my officers, to advise, who with me all agreed that it would be well that they themselves should choose twenty of their number for whom they would be answerable viz: ten of the inhabitants of Grand Pré and village and other ten of the river Cannard inhabitants and they to acquaint the families of their districts how matters were and to assure them that the women and children should be in safety in their absence in their habitations and that it was expected the party indulged should take care to bring in an exact account of their absent brethren and their circumstances on the morrow. . . .

September 5th. The French people not having any provisions with them and pleading hunger begged for bread on which I gave them. And ordered that for the future they be supplied from their respective families. Thus ended the memorable fifth of September, a day of great fatigue and trouble. . . .

1755, September 7. Proved a very busy day, advice arrived from every quarter which I answered as well as I could in the foregoing letters. The French remained in quiet. We mounted guard with half our party, Captain Adams and Osgood doing duty by turns. Captain Hobbs sick. We all lay on our arms since detaining the French here. Kept a good look out and I not wanting in turning out at all times when I awoke so that I was on both watches. . . .

September 10. The French this morning discovered some uncommon motions among themselves which I did not like. Called my officers together and communicated to them what I had observed, and after debating matters it was determined, nemo contra dissente, that it would be best to divide the prisoners, and that as there were five transports idle which came from Boston, it would be for the good of his Majesty's service and that it tended to the better security of the whole, that fifty men of the French inhabitants be embarked on board each of the five vessels, taking first all their young men, and that Captain Adams in the Warren be desired and directed as he was a vessel of force and in his Majesty's service to take the transports under his directions and when the prisoners

were embarked to give such orders to the masters of
the transports as would be best for his Majesty's service, and also determined that six non-commissioned
officers or private men be put on board each transport
as a guard and that Captain Adams and the masters
be immediately ordered to get things in readiness for
that service after which I sent for Father Landrey their
principal speaker who talks English and told him the
time was come for part of the inhabitants to embark
and that the number concluded for this day was 250
and that we should begin with the young men and
desired he would inform his brethren of it.

He was greatly surprised.  I told him it must be
done and that I should order the whole prisoners to
be drawn up six deep, their young men on the left,
and as the tide in a very little time favored, my design
could not give them above an hour to prepare for
going on board, and ordered our whole party to be
under arms and post themselves between the two
gates and the church in the rear of my quarters, which
was obeyed, and agreeable to my directions.  The
whole of the French inhabitants were drawn together
in one body, their young men as directed on the left.
I then ordered Captain Adams with a Lieutenant 80
non-commissioned officers and private men to draw
off from the main body to guard the young men of
the French amounting to 141 men to the transports
and order the prisoners to march.  They all answered
they would not go without their fathers.  I told them
that was a word I did not understand for that the

King's command was to me absolute and should be absolutely obeyed and that I did not love to use harsh means but that time did not admit of parleys or delays and then ordered the whole troop to fix their bayonets and advance towards the French, and bid the 4 right-hand files of the prisoners, consisting of 24 men which I told off myself to divide from the rest, one of whom I took hold on (who opposed the marching) and bid march. He obeyed and the rest followed though slowly, and went off praying, singing and crying, being met by the women and children all the way (which is 1½ mile) with great lamentations upon their knees praying &c.

I then ordered the remaining French to choose out 109 of their married men to follow their young people (the ice being broken) they readily complied and drew up in a body as said the number, who, upon Captain Adams' return, I ordered off under a guard commanded by Captain Osgood: one subaltern 80 non-commissioned officers and private men who marched them off, but when he came to put them on board the vessels found them but 89 instead of 109. So that the number embarked was but 230, and thus ended this troublesome job, which was a scene of sorrow. After this Captain Adams with the transports fell down from Gaspereau and anchored in the mouth of that river and Piziquid. . . .

# WOLFE DEFEATS MONTCALM AT QUEBEC

*By Captain John Knox*

*THE victory of the Anglo-American forces under General James Wolfe and the capture of Quebec from the French under Montcalm, in 1759, was one of the most important events in modern history. John Fiske asserts that "it marks the greatest turning point yet discovered in modern history." This importance came from the fact that the battle decided for North America that its civilization should be English rather than French.*

*Captain Knox, from whose "journal" this account is taken, was an English naval officer who accompanied the expedition against the French in Canada and was an eye-witness of the events recorded.*

*The night before the battle General Wolfe read aloud to some of his officers Gray's "Elegy Written in a Country Churchyard," and announced in conclusion: "Gentlemen, I would rather have written those lines than to capture Quebec tomorrow."*

GREAT preparations are making throughout the fleet and army to surprise the enemy, and compel them to decide the fate of Quebec by a battle. All the long-boats below the town are to be filled with seamen, marines, and such detachments as can be spared from Points Levi and Orleans, in order to make a feint off Beauport and the Point de Lest, and endeavor to engross the attention of the Sieur de Montcalm, while the army are to force a descent on this side of the town. The Officer of our regiment who commanded the escort yesterday on the reconnoitring party, being asked in the General's hearing, after the health of one of the gentlemen who was reported to be ill, replied "he was

in a very low indifferent state," which the other lamented, saying, "He has but a puny, delicate constitution." This struck his Excellency, it being his own
case, who interrupted, "Don't tell me of constitution;
that officer has good spirits, and good spirits will carry
a man through everything."

A soldier of the Royal Americans deserted this day
[September 12, 1759] from the south shore, and one
came over to us from the enemy, who informed the
General "that he belonged to a detachment composed
of two officers and fifty men who had been sent across
the river to take a prisoner; that the French generals
suspect we are going higher up to lay waste the country and destroy such ships and craft as they have got
above; and that Monsieur Montcalm will not be prevailed on to quit his situation, insisting that the flower
of our army are still below the town; that the reduction of Niagara has caused great discontent in the
French army, that the wretched Canadians are much
dissatisfied, and that Monsieur de Levis is certainly
marched, with a detachment of the army, to Montreal,
in order to reënforce Bourlemacque and stop General
Amherst's progress." This fellow added "that, if we
were fairly landed on the north side of the river, an
incredible number of the French regulars would
actually desert to us." . . .

Before daybreak this morning [September 13] we
made a descent upon the north shore, about half a
quarter of a mile to the eastward of Sillery; and the
light troops were fortunately by the rapidity of the

current carried lower down between us and Cape Diamond. We had in this debarkation thirty flat-bottomed boats, containing about sixteen hundred men. This was a great surprise on the enemy, who from the natural strength of the place did not suspect, and consequently were not prepared against so bold an attempt. The chain of sentries which they had posted along the summit of the heights galled us a little, and picked off several men and some officers before our light infantry got up to dislodge them. This grand enterprise was conducted and executed with great good order and discretion.

As fast as we landed, the boats put off for reënforcements, and the troops formed with much regularity. The General, with Brigadiers Monckton and Murray, was ashore with the first division. We lost no time here, but clambered up one of the steepest precipices that can be conceived, being almost a perpendicular, and of an incredible height. As soon as we gained the summit, all was quiet, and not a shot was heard, owing to the excellent conduct of the light infantry under Colonel Howe. It was by this time clear daylight. Here we formed again, the river and the south country in our rear, our right extending to the town, our left to Sillery, and halted a few minutes. The general then detached the light troops to our left to rout the enemy from their battery, and to disable their guns, except they could be rendered serviceable to the party who were to remain there; and this service was soon performed. We then faced to the right,

and marched toward the town by files till we came
to the Plains of Abraham, an even piece of ground
which General Wolfe had made choice of, while we
stood forming upon the hill. Weather showery.
About six o'clock the enemy first made their appearance upon the heights between us and the town,
whereupon we halted and wheeled to the right,
thereby forming the line of battle. . . .

The enemy had now likewise formed the line of
battle, and got some cannon to play on us, with round
and canister shot; but what galled us most was a body
of Indians and other marksmen they had concealed
in the corn opposite to the front of our right wing,
and a coppice that stood opposite to our center inclining toward our left. But Colonel Hale, by Brigadier Monckton's orders, advanced some platoons
alternately from the forty-seventh regiment, which
after a few rounds obliged these skulkers to retire.
We were now ordered to lie down, and remained some
time in this position. About eight o'clock we had two
pieces of short brass six-pounders playing on the
enemy, which threw them into some confusion, and
obliged them to alter their disposition; and Montcalm
formed them into three large columns. About nine
the two armies moved a little nearer each other. The
light cavalry made a faint attempt upon our parties
at the battery of Sillery, but were soon beat off; and
Monsieur de Bougainville, with his troops from Cape
Rouge, came down to attack the flank of our second
line, hoping to penetrate there. But, by a masterly

disposition of Brigadier Townshend, they were forced to desist; and the third battalion of Royal Americans was then detached to the first ground we had formed on after we gained the heights, to preserve the communication with the beach and our boats.

About ten o'clock the enemy began to advance briskly in three columns, with loud shouts and recovered arms, two of them inclining to the left of our army, and the third toward our right, firing obliquely at the two extremities of our line, from the distance of one hundred and thirty, until they came within forty yards, which our troops withstood with the greatest intrepidity and firmness, still reserving their fire and paying the strictest obedience to their officers. This uncommon steadiness, together with the havoc which the grape-shot from our field-pieces made among them, threw them into some disorder, and was most critically maintained by a well-timed, regular, and heavy discharge of our small arms, such as they could no longer oppose. Hereupon they gave way, and fled with precipitation, so that by the time the cloud of smoke was vanished our men were again loaded, and, profiting by the advantage we had over them, pursued them almost to the gates of the town and the bridge over the little river, redoubling our fire with great eagerness, making many officers and men prisoners.

The weather cleared up, with a comfortably warm sunshine. The Highlanders chased them vigorously

toward Charles River, and the fifty-eighth to the
suburb close to John's gate, until they were checked
by the cannon from the two ships. At the same time
a gun which the town had brought to bear upon us
with grape-shot galled the progress of the regiments
to the right, who were likewise pursuing with equal
ardor, while Colonel Hunt Walsh, by a very judicious
movement, wheeled the battalions of Bragg and Kennedy to the left, and flanked the coppice where a body
of the enemy made a stand as if willing to renew the
action; but a few platoons from these corps completed our victory. Then it was that Brigadier Townshend came up, called off the pursuers, ordered the
whole line to dress and recover their former ground.

Our joy at this success is inexpressibly damped by
the loss we sustained of one of the greatest heroes
which this or any other age can boast of,—General
James Wolfe,—who received his mortal wound as
he was exerting himself at the head of the grenadiers
of Louisburg; and Brigadier Monckton was unfortunately wounded upon the left of the Forty-third and
right of the Forty-seventh Regiment at much the same
time, whereby the command devolved on Brigadier
Townshend, who, with Brigadier Murray, went to
the head of every regiment and returned thanks for
their extraordinary good behavior, congratulating the
officers on our success. There is one incident very
remarkable, and which I can affirm from my own personal knowledge,—that the enemy were extremely
apprehensive of being rigorously treated; for, con-

scious of their inhuman behavior to our troops upon a former occasion, the officers who fell into our hands most piteously (with hats off) sued for quarter, repeatedly declaring they were not at Fort William Henry (called by them Fort George) in the year 1757. A soldier of the Royal Americans who deserted from us this campaign, and fought against us to-day, was found wounded on the field of battle. He was immediately tried by a general court-martial, and was shot to death pursuant to his sentence.

While the two armies were engaged this morning, there was an incessant firing between the town and our south batteries. By the time our troops had taken a little refreshment, a quantity of intrenching tools were brought ashore, and the regiments were employed in redoubting our ground and landing some cannon and ammunition. The officers who are prisoners say that Quebec will surrender in a few days. Some deserters who came out to us in the evening agree in that opinion, and inform us that the Sieur de Montcalm is dying, in great agony, of a wound he received to-day in their retreat.

Thus has our late renowned commander by his superior eminence in the art of war, and a most judicious coup d'état, made a conquest of this fertile, healthy, and hitherto formidable country, with a handful of troops only, in spite of the political schemes and most vigorous efforts of the famous Montcalm, and many other officers of rank and experience at the head of an army considerably more numerous. My pen is too feeble to draw the character of this British Achilles; but the same may, with justice, be said of him as was said of Henry IV. of France: he was possessed of courage, humanity, clemency, generosity, affability, and politeness. . . .

Last night Brigadier Townshend went with a detachment of two hundred men to the French general hospital, situated on the river Charles, and about a mile from the town. This is a convent of nuns of the Augustine Order, who—from principles of charity and piety—take care of all sick and wounded men and officers. Lands are appropriated for the support of this institution, besides which the French king endows it with a yearly salary; and a table is kept there at his expense for convalescent officers, directors, surgeons, apothecaries, etc. The Brigadier found an officer's guard at the convent, but he immediately took possession of the place by posting a captain's command there. The unfortunate Marquis de Montcalm was then in the house, dying of his wound, attended by the bishop and his chaplains. A transport, a schooner, and a parcel of boats, with ordnance and stores, passed the town last night. The enemy fired briskly on them, but without any effect. The garrison appear to be at work upon their ramparts, as if resolved to prolong the siege. Some deserters who came out to us this day inform us that Monsieur de Levis, who has rejoined and collected their shattered forces, had intended to surprise the rear of our camp at daybreak this morning, but upon reconnoitring our situation and finding we had made such excellent use of our time in erecting redoubts and other works, prudently declined the undertaking.

The Sieur de Montcalm died late last night. When his wound was dressed and he settled in bed, the surgeons who attended him were desired to acquaint him ingenuously with their sentiments of him; and, being answered that his wound was mortal, he calmly replied, "he was glad of it." His Excellency then demanded "whether he could survive it long, and how long." He was told, "About a dozen hours, perhaps more, peradventure less." "So much the better," rejoined the eminent warrior. "I am happy I shall not live to see the surrender of Quebec." He then ordered his secretary into the room to adjust his private affairs, which, as soon as they were dispatched, he was visited by Monsieur de Ramsey, the French King's lieutenant, and by other principal officers who desired to receive his Excellency's commands, with the farther measures to be pursued for the defense of Quebec, the capital of Canada. To this the Marquis made the following answer: "I'll neither give orders nor interfere any farther. I have much business that must be attended to, of greater moment than your ruined garrison and this wretched country. My time is very short, therefore pray leave me. I wish you all comfort, and to be happily extricated from your present perplexities." He then called for his chaplain, who, with the bishop of the colony, remained with him till he expired. Some time before this great man departed, we are assured he paid us this compliment: "Since it was my misfortune to be discomfited, and mortally wounded, it is a great consolation to me to be vanquished by so brave and generous an enemy. If I could survive this wound, I would engage to beat three times the number of such forces as I commanded this morning with a third of their number of British troops." . . .

After our late worthy General of renowned memory was carried off wounded to the rear of the front line, he desired those who were about him to lay him down. Being asked if he would have a surgeon, he replied, "It is needless: it is all over with me." One of them then cried out, "They run, see how they run!" "Who runs?" demanded our hero with great earnestness, like a person roused from sleep. The officers answered: "The enemy, sir. Egad, they give way everywhere." Thereupon the General rejoined: "Go, one of you, my lads, to Colonel Burton—; tell him to march Webb's regiment with all speed down to Charles River, to cut off the retreat of the fugitives from the bridge." Then, turning on his side, he added, "Now, God be praised, I will die in peace!" and thus expired.

# THE HUTCHINSON RIOT OVER THE STAMP ACT

*By Josiah Quincy, Jr.*

*THIS instance of the temper of the colonies with regard to the Stamp Act has served to keep alive the name of Thomas Hutchinson, the last royal Governor of the Province of Massachusetts Bay. As its Chief Justice he opposed the obnoxious Act, and later advised its repeal, but he accepted its legality and thereby was mobbed. His pro-British administration as Governor intensified the friction with the patriots, and his other acts hurried the appointment of a military governor for the colony.*

*Quincy, from whose diary this record [dated August 27, 1765] was taken, was a young Boston lawyer when rebellion in the colonies was coming to a head. In the first sessions of Congress he opposed the policies of Jefferson and Madison, declaring that the Louisiana Purchase was a sufficient cause for the dissolution of the Union. This was the first announcement on the floor of Congress of the doctrine of secession.*

THERE cannot, perhaps, be found in the records of time a more flagrant instance to what a pitch of infatuation an incensed populace may arise than last night afforded. The destructions, demolitions, and ruins caused by the rage of the colonies in general—perhaps too justly inflamed —at that singular and ever-memorable statute called the Stamp Act, will make the present year one of the most remarkable eras in the annals of North America. And that peculiar inflammation, which fired the breasts of the people of New England in particular, will always distinguish them as the warmest lovers of liberty; though undoubtedly, in the fury of revenge against those who they thought had disclaimed the name of sons, for that of enslavers and oppressive tax-masters of their native country, they committed acts totally unjustifiable.

The populace of Boston, about a week since, had given a very notable instance of their detestation of the above unconstitutional Act, and had sufficiently shown in what light they viewed the man who would undertake to be the stamp distributor. But, not content with this, the last night they again assembled in King's Street; where, after having kindled a fire, they proceeded, in two separate bodies, to attack the houses of two gentlemen of distinction, who, it had been suggested, were accessories to the present burdens; and did great damage in destroying their houses, furniture, &c., and irreparable damage in destroying their papers. Both parties, who before had acted separately, then unitedly proceeded to the Chief-Justice's house, who, not expecting them, was unattended by his friends, who might have assisted, or proved his innocence. In this situation, all his family, it is said, abandoned the house, but himself and his eldest daughter, whom he repeatedly begged to depart: but as he found all ineffectual, and her resolution fixed to stay and share his fate, with a tumult of passions only to be imagined, he took her in his arms, and carried her to a place of safety, just before the incensed mob arrived. This filial affection saved, it is more than probable, his life. Thus unexpected, and nothing removed from the house, an ample field offered to satiate, if possible, this rage-intoxicated

rabble.  They beset the house on all sides, and soon
destroyed everything of value:—

"Furor arma ministrat."—Virgil.

The destruction was really amazing; for it was equal
to the fury of the onset.  But what above all is to be
lamented is the loss of some of the most valuable
records of the country, and other ancient papers; for,
as his Honor was continuing his history, the oldest
and most important writing and records of the Province, which he had selected with great care, pains, and
expense, were in his possession.  This is a loss greatly
to be deplored, as it is absolutely irretrievable.

The distress a man must feel on such an occasion
can only be conceived by those who the next day saw
his Honor the Chief-Justice come into court, with a
look big with the greatest anxiety, clothed in a manner which would have excited compassion from the
hardest heart, though his dress had not been strik-
ingly contrasted by the other judges and bar, who
appeared in their robes.  Such a man in such a station,
thus habited, with tears starting from his eyes, and
a countenance which strongly told the inward anguish
of his soul,—what must an audience have felt, whose
compassion had before been moved by what they
knew he had suffered, when they heard him pro-
nounce the following words in a manner which the
agitations of his mind dictated?

August Term, 3 George III. in B. R., &c.—Present:
The Hon. Thomas Hutchinson, Esq., Chief-Justice;
John Cushing, Peter Oliver, Esqs., Justices.

The Chief-Justice, addressing the whole court,
said,—

"Gentlemen,—There not being a quorum
of the court without me, I am obliged to appear. Some apology is necessary for my
dress: indeed, I had no other. Destitute of
everything,—no other shirt; no other gar-
ment but what I have on; and not one in my
whole family in a better situation than myself.
The distress of a whole family around me,
young and tender infants hanging about me,
are infinitely more insupportable than what I
feel for myself, though I am obliged to borrow
part of this clothing.

"Sensible that I am innocent, that all the
charges against me are false, I can't help feeling: and though I am not obliged to give an
answer to all the questions that may be put
me by every lawless person, yet I call God to
witness,—and I would not, for a thousand
worlds, call my Maker to witness to falsehood,
—I say, I call my Maker to witness, that I
never, in New England or Old, in Great Britain or America, neither directly nor indirectly,
was aiding, assisting, or supporting—in the
least promoting or encouraging—what is com-
monly called the Stamp Act; but, on the contrary, did all in my power, and strove as much
as in me lay, to prevent it. This is not declared

through timidity; for I have nothing to fear.
They can only take away my life, which is of
but little value when deprived of all its comforts, all that was dear to me, and nothing surrounding me but the most piercing distress.

"I hope the eyes of the people will be
opened, that they will see how easy it is for
some designing, wicked man to spread false
reports, to raise suspicions and jealousies in
the minds of the populace, and enrage them
against the innocent; but, if guilty, this is not
the way to proceed. The laws of our country
are open to punish those who have offended.
This destroying all peace and order of the community,—all will feel its effects; and I hope all
will see how easily the people may be deluded,
inflamed, and carried away with madness
against an innocent man.

"I pray God give us better hearts!"

The court was tnen adjourned, on account of the
riotous disorders of the preceding night, and universal
confusion of the town, to the 15th of October following.

# PITT'S PROTEST AGAINST THE STAMP ACT

*By William Pitt, Later Earl of Chatham*

*THIS address, one of the last made by William Pitt in the House of Commons before he was raised to the peerage, echoed the strong opposition of many Englishmen to taxing the American colonies oppressively, and shows how far the whole question involved the relative rights of the Crown and Parliament in England. Pitt was nothing if not patriotic; indeed, it was his intense love of country that inspired his condemnation of the Stamp Act, in which he foresaw disaster to Britain.*

*When France came to the aid of the colonies, causing such alarm in England as to raise a popular outcry against continuing the war, Pitt, then Earl of Chatham, in a powerful address in the House of Lords protested against the disruption of the Empire and the implied subjugation of Britain by France. It was his last effort; at its conclusion he sank to the floor exhausted, and died a few days later.*

GENTLEMEN, Sir (to the Speaker), I have been charged with giving birth to sedition in America. They have spoken their sentiments with freedom against this unhappy act, and that freedom has become their crime. Sorry I am to hear the liberty of speech in this House imputed as a crime. But the imputation shall not discourage me. It is a liberty I mean to exercise. No gentleman ought to be afraid to exercise it. It is a liberty by which the gentleman who calumniates it might have profited. He ought to have desisted from his project. The gentleman tells us, America is obstinate; America is almost in open rebellion. I rejoice that America has resisted. Three millions of people so dead to all the feelings of liberty, as voluntarily to submit to be

77

slaves, would have been fit instruments to make slaves of the rest. I come not here armed at all points, with law cases and acts of Parliament, with the statute-book doubled down in dog's ears, to defend the cause of liberty: if I had, I myself would have cited the two cases of Chester and Durham. I would have cited them, to have shown that, even under former arbitrary reigns, Parliaments were ashamed of taxing a people without their consent, and allowed them representatives. . . . The gentleman tells us of many who are taxed, and are not represented.—The India Company, merchants, stockholders, manufacturers. Surely many of these are represented in other capacities, as owners of land, or as freemen of boroughs. It is a misfortune that more are not equally represented. But they are all inhabitants, and as such, are they not virtually represented? Many have it in their option to be actually represented. They have connections with those that elect, and they have influence over them. . . .

. . . The gentleman boasts of his bounties to America! Are not these bounties intended finally for the benefit of this kingdom? If they are not, he has misapplied the national treasures. I am no courtier of America—I stand up for this kingdom. I maintain, that the Parliament has a right to bind, to restrain America. Our legislative power over the colonies is sovereign and supreme. When it ceases to be sovereign and supreme, I would advise every gentleman to sell his lands, if he can, and embark for that country.

When two countries are connected together, like England and her colonies, without being incorporated, the one must necessarily govern; the greater must rule the less; but so rule it, as not to contradict the fundamental principles that are common to both.

If the gentleman does not understand the difference between external and internal taxes, I cannot help it; but there is a plain distinction between taxes levied for the purposes of raising a revenue, and duties imposed for the regulation of trade, for the accommodation of the subject; although, in the consequences, some revenue might incidentally arise from the latter.

The gentleman asks, when were the colonies emancipated? But I desire to know, when they were made slaves? But I dwell not upon words. When I had the honor of serving his Majesty, I availed myself of the means of information, which I derived from my office: I speak, therefore, from knowledge. My materials were good, I was at pains to collect, to digest, to consider them; and I will be bold to affirm, that the profits to Great Britain from the trade of the colonies, through all its branches, is two millions a year. This is the fund that carried you triumphantly through the last war. The estates that were rented at two thousand pounds a year, threescore years ago, are at three thousand pounds at present. Those estates sold then from fifteen to eighteen years purchase; the same may now be sold for thirty. You owe this to America. This is the price America pays for her protection. And shall a miserable financier come with a boast, that he can bring a pepper-corn into the exchequer, to the loss of millions to the nation! I dare not say, how much higher these profits may be augmented. Omitting the immense increase of people by natural population, in the northern colonies, and the emigration from every part of Europe, I am convinced the commercial system of America may be altered to advantage. You have prohibited where you ought to have encouraged, and encouraged where you ought to have prohibited. . . .

A great deal has been said without doors, of the power, of the strength of America. It is a topic that ought to be cautiously meddled with. In a good cause, on a sound bottom, the force of this country can crush America to atoms. I know the valor of your troops. I know the skill of your officers. There is not a company of foot that has served in America, out of which you may not pick a man of sufficient knowledge and experience to make a governor of a colony there. But on this ground, on the Stamp Act, when so many here will think it a crying injustice, I am one who will lift up my hands against it.

In such a cause, your success would be hazardous. America, if she fell, would fall like the strong man. She would embrace the pillars of the state, and pull down the constitution along with her. Is this your boasted peace? Not to sheath the sword in its scabbard, but to sheath it in the bowels of your countrymen? Will you quarrel with yourselves, now the whole House of Bourbon is united against you? . . .

THE OLD STATE HOUSE, BOSTON, MASSACHUSETTS. THE ROSETTE MARKS
THE SPOT WHERE THE BOSTON MASSACRE OCCURRED, MARCH 5, 1770

The Americans have not acted in all things with prudence and temper. The Americans have been wronged. They have been driven to madness by injustice. Will you punish them for the madness you have occasioned? Rather let prudence and temper come first from this side. I will undertake for America, that she will follow the example. There are two lines in a ballad of Prior's, of a man's behavior to his wife, so applicable to you, and your colonies, that I cannot help repeating them:

> Be to her faults a little blind:
> Be to her virtues very kind.

Upon the whole, I will beg leave to tell the House what is really my opinion. It is, that the Stamp Act be repealed absolutely, totally, and immediately. That the reason for the repeal be assigned, because it was founded on an erroneous principle. At the same time, let the sovereign authority of this country over the colonies be asserted in as strong terms as can be devised, and be made to extend to every point of legislation whatsoever. That we may bind their trade, confine their manufactures, and exercise every power whatsoever, except that of taking their money out of their pockets without their consent.

# THE REPEAL OF THE STAMP ACT

*By Secretary Henry Seymour Conway*

CONWAY was one of the two English Secretaries of State in 1766 when he wrote this official communication to the governors of the American colonies. Incidentally, he persistently opposed the war with America, and in 1782, in an address to Parliament, urged the advisability of discontinuing the struggle. This is particularly interesting in view of the fact that, during the same year, he succeeded Lord North as Commander-in-Chief of the British army.

Receipt of this communication from the mother country was the signal for great rejoicing throughout the colonies, though dissatisfaction was soon expressed with regard to the Declaratory Act asserting a right to "bind the colonies and people of America . . . in all cases whatsoever." The whole affair has been regarded as one of the chief causes of the Revolution.

HEREWITH I have the pleasure of transmitting to you copies of two acts of Parliament just passed. The first for securing the dependency of the colonies on the mother country; the second for the repeal of the act of [the] last session, granting certain stamp duties in America; and I expect shortly to send you a third, for the indemnity of such persons, as have incurred the penalties imposed by the act just repealed, as such a bill is now depending, and has made a considerable progress in the House of Commons.

The moderation, the forbearance, the unexampled lenity and tenderness of Parliament towards the colonies, which are so signally displayed in those acts, cannot but dispose the province, committed to your care, to that return of cheerful obedience to the laws and legislative authority of Great Britain and to those sentiments of respectful gratitude to the mother country, which are the natural, and I trust, will be the certain effects of so much grace and condescension, so remarkably manifested on the part of his Majesty and of the Parliament; and the future happiness and prosperity of the colonies will very much depend on the testimonies they shall now give of these dispositions.

For, as a dutiful and affectionate return to such peculiar proofs of indulgence and affection, may, now at this great crisis, be a means of fixing the mutual interests and inclinations of Great Britain and her colonies on the most firm and solid foundations, so it cannot but appear visible that the least coldness or unthankfulness, the least murmuring or dissatisfaction on any ground whatever, of former heat, or too much prevailing prejudice, may fatally endanger that union, and give the most severe and affecting blow to the future interests of both countries.

You will think it scarcely possible, I imagine, that the paternal care of His Majesty for his colonies, or the lenity or indulgence of the Parliament should go further than I have already mentioned: yet, so full of true magnanimity are the sentiments of both, and so free from the smallest color of passion or prejudice that they seem disposed not only to forgive, but to forget those most unjustifiable marks of an undutiful disposition too frequent in the late transactions of the colonies, and which, for the honor of those colonies, it were to be wished had been more discountenanced and discouraged by those, who had knowledge to conduct themselves otherwise.

A revision of the late American Trade Laws is going to be the immediate object of Parliament; nor will the late transactions there, however provoking, prevent, I dare say, the full operation of that kind and indulgent disposition prevailing both in His Majesty and his Parliament to give to the trade and interests of America every relief which the true state of their circumstances demands or admits. Nothing will tend more effectually to every conciliating purpose, and there is nothing therefore I have it in command more earnestly to require of you, than that you should exert yourself in recommending it strongly to the assembly, that full and ample compensation be made to those, who, from the madness of the people, have suffered for their deference to acts of the British legislature; and you will be particularly attentive that such persons be effectually secured from any further insults; and that as far as in you lies, you will take care, by your example and influence, that they may be treated with that respect to their persons, and that justice in regard to all their pretensions, which their merit and their sufferings undoubtedly claim. The resolutions of the House of Commons, which, by His Majesty's commands I transmit to you, to be laid before the assembly, will show you the sense of that house on those points; and I am persuaded it will, as it certainly ought, be, the glory of that assembly to adopt and imitate those sentiments of the British Parliament, founded on the clearest principles of humanity and justice. . . .

# AN EYE-WITNESS DESCRIBES THE BOSTON MASSACRE

## By John Tudor

*THE author of this document was a Boston merchant who was in the midst of the stirring events in the New England metropolis from 1732 to 1793. The soldiers involved in the so-called massacre were indicted for murder, were defended by John Adams, and were acquitted, though two of them were declared guilty of manslaughter and received light punishments.*

*There is much difference of opinion about the event, some writers regarding it as a lawless affair discreditable to the people and soldiers alike and without any great historical significance; others, including John Adams, look upon it as the "first act in the drama of the Revolution."*

ON Monday evening the 5th current, a few minutes after 9 o'clock a most horrid murder was committed in King Street before the Customhouse door by 8 or 9 soldiers under the command of Captain Thomas Preston, drawn off from the main guard on the south side of the Townhouse.

This unhappy affair began by some boys and young fellows throwing snow balls at the sentry placed at the Customhouse door. On which 8 or 9 soldiers came to his assistance. Soon after a number of people collected, when the Captain commanded the soldiers to fire, which they did and 3 men were killed on the spot and several mortally wounded, one of whom died the next morning. The Captain soon drew off his soldiers up to the main guard, or the consequences might have been terrible, for on the guns firing the people were alarmed and set the bells a-ringing as if for fire, which drew multitudes to the place of action. Lieutenant Governor Hutchinson, who was commander-in-chief, was sent for and came to the council chamber, where some of the magistrates attended. The Governor desired the multitude about 10 o'clock to separate and go home peaceably and he would do all in his power that justice should be done, etc. The 29th regiment being then under arms on the south side of the Townhouse, but the people insisted that the soldiers should be ordered to their barracks first before they would separate, which being done the people separated about one o'clock. Captain Preston was taken up by a warrant given to the high Sheriff by Justice Dania and Tudor and came under examination about 2 o'clock and we sent him to jail soon after 3, having evidence sufficient to commit him on his ordering the soldiers to fire. So about 4 o'clock the town became quiet. The next forenoon the 8 soldiers that fired on the inhabitants were also sent to jail. Tuesday A.M. the inhabitants met at Faneuil Hall and after some pertinent speeches, chose a committee of 15 gentlemen to wait on the Lieutenant Governor in council to request the immediate removal of the troops. The message was in these words: That it is the unanimous opinion of this meeting, that the inhabitants and soldiery can no longer live together in safety; that nothing can rationally be expected to restore the peace of the town and prevent blood and carnage but the removal of the troops; and that we most fervently pray his honor that his power and influence may be exerted for their instant removal. His honor's reply was, "Gentlemen I am extremely sorry for the unhappy difference and especially of the last evening," and signifying that it was not in his power to remove the troops, &c., &c.

The above reply was not satisfactory to the inhabitants, as but one regiment should be removed to the castle barracks. In the afternoon the town adjourned to Dr. Sewill's meetinghouse, for Faneuil Hall was not large enough to hold the people, there being at least 3,000, some supposed near 4,000, when they chose a committee to wait on the Lieutenant Governor to let him and the council know that nothing less will satisfy the people, than a total and immediate removal of the troops out of the town. His honor laid before the council the vote of the town. The council thereon expressed themselves to be unanimously of opinion that it was absolutely necessary for his Majesty's service, the good order of the town, &c., that the troops should be immediately removed out of the town. His honor communicated this advice of the council to Colonel Dalrymple and desired he would order the troops down to castle William. After the Colonel had seen the vote of the council he gave his word and honor to the town's committee that both the regiments should be removed without delay. The committee returned to the town meeting and Mr. Hancock, chairman of the committee, read their report as above, which was received with a shout and clap of hands, which made the meetinghouse ring. So the meeting was dissolved and a great number of gentlemen appeared to watch the center of the town and the prison, which continued for 11 nights and all was quiet again, as the soldiers were moved off to the castle.

(Thursday) Agreeable to a general request of the inhabitants, were followed to the grave (for they were all buried in one) in succession the 4 bodies of Messrs. Samuel Gray, Samuel Maverick, James Caldwell and Crispus Attucks, the unhappy victims who fell in the bloody massacre.  On this sorrowful occasion most of the shops and stores in town were shut, all the bells were ordered to toll a solemn peal in Boston, Charleston, Cambridge and Roxbury.  The several hearses forming a junction in King Street, the theatre of that inhuman tragedy, proceeded from thence through the main street, lengthened by an immense concourse of people, so numerous as to be obliged to follow in ranks of 4 and 6 abreast and brought up by a long train of carriages.  The sorrow visible in the countenances, together with the peculiar solemnity, surpasses description, it was supposed that the spectators and those that followed the corpses amounted to 15,000, some supposed 20,000.  Note Captain Preston was tried for his life on the affair of the above October 24, 1770.  The trial lasted 5 days, but the jury brought him in not guilty.

# DANIEL BOONE MIGRATES TO KENTUCKY

## His Own Account

*BOONE wrote this account, which appears in Hart's "Source Book of American History," many years after his migration. As his schooling was extremely limited, the article was put into literary form by a friend. His life, from the time of his first trip to Kentucky in 1769 to his death in Missouri in 1820, was a constant duel with hardships and Indians.*

*On the site of Boonesboro, Ky., he built a fort and settled his family a year before the Declaration of Independence was signed. Not long afterwards he was captured by the redskins, who took him to Detroit, finally adopted him and allowed him such freedom that he escaped and made his way back to Kentucky on foot, reaching his fort in time to help defend it against a savage attack. Losing his Kentucky lands through defective titles, he settled in Missouri and again became landless through Government litigation.*

IT WAS on the first of May, in the year 1769, that I resigned my domestic happiness for a time, and left my family and peaceable habitation on the Yadkin River, in North Carolina, to wander through the wilderness of America, in quest of the country of Kentucky, in company with John Finley, John Stewart, Joseph Holden, James Monay, and William Cool.

We proceeded successfully, and after a long and tiresome journey through a mountainous wilderness, in a westward direction, on the seventh day of June following, we found ourselves on Red River, where John Finley had formerly gone trading with the Indians; and, from the top of an eminence, saw with pleasure the beautiful level of Kentucky.

We found everywhere abundance of wild beasts of all sorts, through this vast forest. The buffalo were more frequent than I have seen cattle in the settlements, browsing on the leaves of the cane, or cropping the herbage on those extensive plains, fearless, because ignorant of the violence of man. Sometimes we saw hundreds in a drove, and the numbers about the salt springs were amazing.

As we ascended the brow of a small hill, near Kentucky River, a number of Indians rushed out of a thick cane-brake upon us, and made us prisoners. The time of our sorrow was now arrived, and the scene fully opened. They plundered us of what we had, and kept us in confinement seven days, treating us with common savage usage. During this time we showed no uneasiness or desire to escape, which made them less suspicious of us. But in the dead of night, as we lay in a thick cane-brake by a large fire, when sleep had locked up their senses, my situation not disposing me for rest, I touched my companion and gently woke him.

We improved this favorable opportunity, and departed, leaving them to take their rest, and speedily directed our course toward our old camp, but found it plundered, and the company dispersed and gone home.

Soon after this my companion in captivity, John Stewart, was killed by the savages, and the man that came with my brother returned home by himself. We were then in a dangerous, helpless situation, exposed daily to perils and death among savages and wild beasts, not a white man in the country but ourselves.

One day I undertook a tour through the country, and the diversity and beauties of nature I met with in this charming season expelled every gloomy and vexatious thought. I laid me down to sleep, and I awoke not until the sun had chased away the night. I continued this tour, and in a few days explored a considerable part of the country, each day equally pleased as the first.

I returned again to my old camp, which was not disturbed in my absence. I did not confine my lodging to it, but often reposed in thick cane-brakes to avoid the savages, who, I believe, often visited my camp, but fortunately for me, in my absence. In this situation I was constantly exposed to danger and death. How unhappy such a situation for a man! Tormented with fear, which is vain if no danger comes. The prowling wolves diverted my nocturnal hours with perpetual howlings.

In 1772 I returned safe to my old home, and found my family in happy circumstances. I sold my farm on the Yadkin, and what goods we could not carry with us; and on the twenty-fifth day of September, 1773, bade a farewell to our friends and proceeded on our journey to Kentucky, in company with five families more, and forty men that joined us in Powel's Valley, which is one hundred and fifty miles from the now settled parts of Kentucky.

This promising beginning was soon overcast with a cloud of adversity; for upon the tenth day of October the rear of our company was attacked by a number of Indians, who killed six and wounded one man. Of these my eldest son was one that fell in the action.

Though we defended ourselves, and repulsed the enemy, yet this unhappy affair scattered our cattle, brought us into extreme difficulty, and so discouraged the whole company that we retreated forty miles to the settlement on Clench River.

Within fifteen miles of where Boonsborough now stands we were fired upon by a party of Indians that killed two and wounded two of our number; yet although surprised and taken at a disadvantage, we stood our ground. This was on the twentieth of March, 1775.

Three days after we were fired upon again, and had two men killed and three wounded. Afterward we proceeded on to Kentucky River without opposition; and on the first day of April began to erect the fort of Boonsborough at a salt lick, about sixty yards from the river, on the south side. On the fourth day the Indians killed one man.

In a short time I proceeded to remove my family from Clench to this garrison, where we arrived safe without any other difficulties than such as are common to this passage, my wife and daughter being the first white women that ever stood on the banks of Kentucky River. On the twenty-fourth day of December following we had one man killed and one wounded by the Indians, who seemed determined to persecute us for erecting this fortification.

On the fourteenth day of July, 1776, two of Colonel Calaway's daughters and one of mine were taken prisoners near the fort. I immediately pursued the Indians, with only eight men, and on the sixteenth overtook them, killed two of the party and recovered the girls. The same day on which this attempt was made the Indians divided themselves into different parties and attacked several forts, which were shortly before this time erected, doing a great deal of mischief. This was extremely distressing to the new settlers. The innocent husbandman was shot down while busy in cultivating the soil for his family's supply. Most of the cattle around the stations were destroyed. They continued their hostilities in this manner until the fifteenth of April, 1777, when they attacked Boonsborough with a party of above one hundred in number, killed one man and wounded four. Their loss in this attack was not certainly known to us.

On the fourth day of July following a party of about two hundred Indians attacked Boonsborough, killed one man and wounded two. They besieged us forty-eight hours; during which time seven of them were killed, and finding themselves not likely to prevail, they raised the siege and departed.

The Indians had disposed their warriors in different parties at this time and attacked the different garrisons to prevent their assisting each other, and did much injury to the inhabitants.

On the nineteenth day of this month Colonel Logan's fort was besieged by a party of about two hundred Indians. During this dreadful siege they did a great deal of mischief, distressed the garrison, in which were only fifteen men, killed two and wounded one.

This campaign in some measure damped the spirits of the Indians, and made them sensible of our superiority. Their connections were dissolved, their armies scattered, and a future invasion put entirely out of their power; yet they continued to practise mischief secretly upon the inhabitants, in the exposed parts of the country.

In October following a party made an excursion into that district called the Crab Orchard, and one of them, who was advanced some distance before the others, boldly entered the house of a poor defenseless family, in which was only a negro man, a woman and her children, terrified with the apprehensions of immediate death. The savage, perceiving their defenseless situation, without offering violence to the family, attempted to captivate the negro, who happily proved an overmatch for him, threw him on the ground, and, in the struggle, the mother of the children drew an ax from a corner of the cottage and cut his head off, while her little daughter shut the door. The savages instantly appeared, and applied their tomahawks to the door. An old rusty gun-barrel, without a lock, lay in a corner, which the mother put through a small crevice, and the savages, perceiving it, fled. In the mean time the alarm spread through the neighborhood; the armed men collected immediately, and pursued the ravagers into the wilderness. Thus Providence, by the means of this negro, saved the whole of the poor family from destruction. From that time until the happy return of peace between the United States and Great Britain the Indians did us no mischief.

To conclude, I can now say that I have verified the saying of an old Indian who signed Colonel Henderson's deed. Taking me by the hand, at the delivery thereof, "Brother," says he, "we have given you a fine land, but I believe you will have much trouble in settling it." My footsteps have often been marked with blood, and therefore I can truly subscribe to its original name. Two darling sons, and a brother, have I lost by savage hands, which have also taken from me forty valuable horses and abundance of cattle. Many dark and sleepless night have I been a companion for owls, separated from the cheerful society of men, scorched by the summer's sun, and pinched by the winter's cold, an instrument ordained to settle the wilderness. But now the scene is changed: peace crowns the sylvan shade.

# THE BOSTON TEA PARTY

*By Thomas Hutchinson*

*GOVERNOR HUTCHIN-SON, from whose history of Massachusetts Bay this account of the Boston Tea Party exploit is taken, has been criticized for not ordering the tea-laden ships back to England, as was done in Philadelphia and New York, but there was a shortage of tea that winter of 1773 in New England and, we are assured, "the merchants would never have submitted to the disappointment and loss." The tea in question was consigned, among others, to two sons of the Governor and to Benjamin Faneuil, whose name is commemorated in Faneuil Hall.*

*It is noteworthy that Hutchinson's biographer, James K. Hosmer, is also the most popular biographer of Samuel Adams. "It was while writing the life of that sturdy Son of Liberty," says Professor Hosmer, "that the worth and greatness of his opponent became plain to me." Hutchinson's estate was confiscated, and later in life he was forced through poverty to decline an English baronetcy.*

THE assembly being prorogued, there was again room to hope for a few months of freedom from civil contention. The complaint against the Governor was gone to England; the salaries of the judges were suspended for the consideration of the next session: these were the two subjects of controversy peculiar to Massachusetts colony. Not more than two or three months had passed before a new subject was brought on, which had its effect in all the colonies, but greater in Massachusetts than in any other.

When the affairs of the East India Company were under the consideration of Parliament, to facilitate the consumption of tea, a vast quantity whereof then lay in the warehouses, it was determined to export a part of it, on account of the

company, to the colonies, there to be sold by factors
at a much lower price than it could be afforded by
particular merchants who purchased it in England.
When the intelligence first came to Boston, it caused
no alarm. The threepenny duty had been paid the
last two years without any stir, and some of the great
friends to liberty had been importers of tea. The body
of the people were pleased with the prospect of drinking tea at less expense than ever. The only apparent
discontent was among the importers of tea, as well
those who had been legal importers from England, as
others who had illegally imported from Holland; and
the complaint was against the East India Company for
monopolizing a branch of commerce which had been
beneficial to a great number of particular merchants.
And the first suggestion of a design in the ministry
to enlarge the revenue, and to habituate the colonies
to parliamentary taxes, was made from England; and
opposition to the measure was recommended, with an
intimation that it was expected that the tea would not
be suffered to be landed. The committees of correspondence in the several colonies soon availed themselves of so favorable an opportunity for promoting
their great purpose. It soon appeared to be their
general determination that, at all events, the tea
should be sent back to England in the ships which
brought it. The first motions were at Philadelphia
where, at a meeting of the people, every man who
should be concerned in unlading, receiving, or vend-
ing the tea was pronounced an enemy to his country.

The example was soon followed at Boston. The people were summoned, by notifications posted in different quarters, to meet at the tree of liberty, to hear the resignation of the consignees of the tea, which was then daily expected. The consignees also, by a letter left at one of their houses, were required to attend at the same time at their peril. The people met, but, the consignees not appearing, a committee was appointed to acquaint them at one of their warehouses where they had met that, as they had neglected to attend, the people thought themselves warranted to consider them as their enemies. . . .

Three vessels were expected every hour with the teas. The consignees were afraid of exposing themselves and their bondsmen to damages, which might arise from a refusal or neglect to execute their trust; on the other hand, they were anxiously concerned for their personal safety, and made their application to the Governor. He foresaw that this would prove a more difficult affair than any which had preceded it since he had been in the chair. The controversies with the council and house had a tendency to deprive him of the esteem and favor of the people; but he had not been apprehensive of injury to his person. He was now to encounter with bodies of the people collected together, and a great proportion of them the lowest part of the people, from whom, when there is no power to restrain them, acts of violence are to be expected. He knew that the council would give him no aid. . . . He considered that, if the ships came

into the harbor above the castle, they could not pass
by it again without a permit under his hand, and that
his granting such permit would be more than he
should be able to justify. He therefore advised to
their anchoring without the castle, and their waiting
for orders; and this advice was approved of by the
consignees, and by the owner of the ship first expected, if not by the owners of the other ships; and
orders were given to the pilots accordingly. . . .

On Sunday one of the ships with the tea arrived,
and anchored below the castle. Notification in a form
proper to inflame the people was posted up, calling
upon them to assemble; and while the Governor and
council were sitting on the Monday in the council
chamber, and known to be consulting upon means for
preserving the peace of the town, several thousands,
inhabitants of Boston and other towns, were assembled in a public meeting-house at a small distance,
in direct opposition and defiance. . . .

The people assembled in Boston took the name of
"the body" instead of a "legal town meeting," and
began with that spirit with which all established
powers ought to act in the exercise of their legal con-
stitutional authority. They resolved that, "at all
events," the tea arrived in [in the ship commanded
by] Captain Hall should be returned to the place from
whence it came, and that no duty should be paid upon
it. They then adjourned to the afternoon, to give
time for the consignees to deliberate. As soon as they
reassembled, they resolved that the tea should be sent

back in the same bottom in which it came. To this resolve the owner of the vessel, who was present in the meeting, said he must enter a protest. It was thereupon resolved that Mr. Rotch, the owner, be directed not to enter the tea, and Captain Hall, the master, not to suffer any of it to be landed, at their peril. They did not stop at mere declaratory acts or naked resolves. This, they knew, would render future acts and resolves contemptible. They established a watch of twenty-five inhabitants for securing the ship and cargo, and appointed a captain for the night. . . .

The consignees, in a letter to the selectmen of Boston, which was read to the meeting, signified that it was utterly out of their power to send the tea back to England, but they would engage to keep it in a store until they could receive further directions from England, to which they afterwards added that they would be content to have it under the constant inspection of a committee, to be appointed by the town. But all was declared not in the least degree satisfactory, and that nothing short of sending back the tea would be so. The owner and master of the ship were directed to attend the "body"; and a vote passed, while they were present, without a negative, "that it is the firm resolution of the body that the owner shall return the tea in the same vessel in which it came, and that they now require it of him." The owner promised to comply, but intimated that it was by compulsion, and that he should be obliged to protest, to save himself from damage. The master also promised to carry it back. . . .

As a permit or pass was always required at the
castle, for all vessels except small coasters, and there
were several men of war in the harbor, which it was
supposed would stop the ship from proceeding any
other way, the destruction of the tea was considered
as necessary to prevent payment of the duty.  A demand was made from the collector, in form, of a
clearance for the ship, which he could not grant until
the goods which were imported, and regularly entered,
were landed, and the duties paid, or secured; and the
like demand of a permit was made of the naval officer, with whom blank permits were intrusted by the
Governor, to be filled up, and delivered to such vessels
only as had been cleared at the custom-house, and,
therefore, in this case was refused.  It was expected
that in twenty days after the arrival of the tea a demand of the duty would be made by the collector, and
the ship or goods be seized; which would occasion
additional difficulties.  Another meeting of the body
was, therefore, called, in order to inquire the reason
of the delay in sending the ship back to England.  The
people came into Boston from the adjacent towns
within twenty miles, from some, more, from others,
less, as they were affected; and, as soon as they were
assembled, enjoined the owner of the ship, at his peril,
to demand of the collector of the customs a clearance
for the ship, and appointed ten of their number a committee to accompany him; and adjourned for two days
to receive the report.  Being reassembled and informed
by the owner that a clearance was refused, he was

then enjoined immediately to apply to the Governor
for a pass by the castle.   He made an apology to the
Governor for coming upon such an errand, having
been compelled to it; and received an answer that no
pass ever had been, or lawfully could be, given to any
vessel which had not first been cleared at the custom-
house, and that, upon his producing a clearance, such
pass would immediately be given by the naval officer.
The Governor inquired of him whether he did not
apprehend his ship in danger from the people, and
offered him a letter to Admiral Montagu, desiring him
to afford all necessary protection.   He said he had
been advised to remove his vessel under the stern of
the admiral's ship, but, among other reasons for not
doing it, mentioned his fears of the rage of the people;
that his concern was not for his ship, which he did not
believe was in danger, but he could not tell what
would be the fate of the tea on board.   He declined
taking any letter to the admiral, and returned to the
people.   The Governor was unable to judge what
would be the next step.   The secretary had informed
him that a principal leader of the people had declared,
in the hearing of the deputy secretary, that, if the
Governor should refuse a pass, he would demand it
himself, at the head of one hundred and fifty men,
&c.; and he was not without apprehensions of a further application.   But he was relieved from his sus-
pense, the same evening, by intelligence from town of
the total destruction of the tea.

It was not expected that the Governor would comply with the demand; and, before it was possible for

the owner of the ship to return from the country with an answer, about fifty men had prepared themselves, and passed by the house where the people were assembled to the wharf where the vessels lay, being covered with blankets, and making the appearance of Indians. The body of the people remained until they had received the Governor's answer; and then, after it had been observed to them that, every thing else in their power having been done, it now remained to proceed in the only way left, and that, the owner of the ship having behaved like a man of honor, no injury ought to be offered to his person or property, the meeting was declared to be dissolved, and the body of the people repaired to the wharf, and surrounded the immediate actors, as a guard and security, until they had finished their work. In two or three hours they hoisted out of the holds of the ships three hundred and forty-two chests of tea, and emptied them into the sea. . . .

The Governor was unjustly censured by many people in the province, and much abused by the pamphlet and newspaper writers in England for refusing his pass, which, it was said, would have saved the property thus destroyed; but he would have been justly censured if he had granted it. . . .

Even the declarations of the Governor against the unlawful invasions of the people upon the authority of government were charged against him as officious, unnecessary acts, and were made to serve to inflame the people and increase disorders. . . .

Notwithstanding the forlorn state he was in, he thought it necessary to keep up some show of authority, and caused a council to be summoned to meet at Boston the day after the destruction of the tea, and went to town himself to be present at it; but a quorum did not attend. The people had not fully recovered from the state of mind which they were in the preceding night. Great pains had been taken to persuade them that the obstructions they had met with, which finally brought on the loss of the tea, were owing to his influence; and, being urged to it by his friends, he left the town, and lodged that night at the castle, under pretence of a visit to his sons, who were confined there with the other consignees of the tea. Failing in an attempt for a council the next day at Milton, he met them, three days after, at Cambridge, where they were much divided in their opinion. One of them declared against any step whatever. The people, he said, had taken the powers of government into their hands,—any attempt to restrain them would only enrage them, and render them more desperate; while another observed that, having done everything else in their power to prevent the tea from being landed, and all to no purpose, they had been driven to the necessity of destroying it, as a less evil than submission to the duty. So many of the actors and abettors were universally known that a proclamation, with a reward for discovery, would have been ridiculed. The attorney-general, therefore, was ordered to lay the matter before the grand jury, who, there was no room to expect, would ever find a bill for what they did not consider as an offence.

This was the boldest stroke which had yet been struck in America. The people in all parts of the province showed more or less concern at the expected consequences. They were, however, at a distance; something might intervene to divert them. Besides, the thing was done: there was no way of nullifying it. Their leaders feared no consequences. To engage the people in some desperate measure had long been their plan. They never discovered more concern than when the people were quiet upon the repeal of an act of Parliament, or upon concessions made, or assurances given; and never more satisfaction than when government had taken any new measures, or appeared to be inclined to them, tending, or which might be improved, to irritate and disturb the people. They had nothing to fear for themselves. They had gone too far to recede. If the colonies were subject to the supreme authority and laws of Great Britain, their offences, long since, had been of the highest nature. Their all depended upon attaining to the object which first engaged them. There was no way of attaining to it but by involving the body of the people in the same circumstances they were in themselves. And it is certain that ever after this time an opinion was easily instilled, and was continually increasing, that the body of the people had also gone too far to recede, and that an open and general revolt must be the consequence; and it was not long before actual preparations were visibly making for it in most parts of the province.

# THE FIRST CONTINENTAL CONGRESS

*By Delegate John Adams*

*THAT John Adams, schoolmaster, lawyer, public man, member of the Continental Congress, diplomat and later Vice-President and President of the United States, was one of the keenest observers of his time is evidenced by this informal report of the sessions of the 1774 Continental Congress in Philadelphia, to which he was one of the five Massachusetts delegates. He modestly refrains from dwelling upon his own activities in the historic body, but his energy was devoted to the adoption of a comprehensive program having three distinct elements—the organization of commonwealth governments on an independent basis, the formation of a national confederate government, and the establishment of diplomatic relations with foreign powers.*

*His success in finally getting the Congress of 1776 to adopt resolutions recommending the formation of permanently independent state governments made the Declaration of Independence natural, if not inevitable. Adams was on the committee which drafted that document.*

AT ten the delegates all met at the City Tavern, and walked to the Carpenters' Hall, where they took a view of the room, and of the chamber where is an excellent library; there is also a long entry where gentlemen may walk, and a convenient chamber opposite to the library. The general cry was that this was a good room, and the question was put, whether we were satisfied with this room? It passed in the affirmative. A very few were for the negative, and they were chiefly from Pennsylvania and New York. Then Mr. Lynch arose, and said there was a gentleman present who had presided with great dignity over a very respectable society, greatly to the advantage of America, and he therefore proposed that the Honorable Peyton Randolph, Esquire, one of the delegates from Virginia, and the late Speaker of their House of Burgesses, should be appointed Chairman, and he doubted not it would be unanimous.

The question was put, and he was unanimously chosen.

Mr. Randolph then took the chair, and the commission of the delegates were all produced and read.

Then Mr. Lynch proposed that Mr. Charles Thomson, a gentleman of family, fortune and character in this city, should be appointed Secretary, which was accordingly done without opposition, though Mr. Duane and Mr. Jay discovered at first an inclination to seek further.

Mr. Duane then moved that a committee should be appointed to prepare regulations for this Congress. Several gentlemen objected.

I then arose and asked leave of the President to request of the gentleman from New York an explanation, and that he would point out some particular regulations which he had in mind. He mentioned particularly the method of voting, whether it should be by colonies, or by the poll, or by interests.

Mr. Henry then arose, and said this was the first general Congress which had ever happened; that no former Congress could be a precedent; that we should have occasion for more general Congresses, and therefore that a precedent ought to be established now; that it would be great injustice if a little colony should have the same weight in the councils of America as a great one, and therefore he was for a committee.

Major Sullivan observed that a little colony had its all at stake as well as a great one. . . .

Mr. Henry. Government is dissolved. Fleets and armies and the present state of things show that government is dissolved. Where are your landmarks, your boundaries of colonies? We are in a state of nature, sir. I did propose that a scale should be laid down; that part of North America which was once Massachusetts Bay, and that part which was once Virginia, ought to be considered as having a weight. Will not people complain? Ten thousand Virginians have not outweighed one thousand others. I will submit, however; I am determined to submit, if I am overruled. A worthy gentleman (ego) near me seemed to admit the necessity of obtaining a more adequate representation. I hope future ages will quote our proceedings with applause. It is one of the great duties of the democratical part of the constitution to keep itself pure. It is known in my province that some other colonies are not so numerous or rich as they are. I am for giving all the satisfaction in my power. The distinctions between Virginians, Pennsylvanians, New Yorkers, and New Englanders, are no more. I am not a Virginian, but an American. Slaves are to be thrown out of the question, and if the freemen can be represented according to their numbers, I am satisfied.

Mr. Lynch. I differ in one point from the gentleman from Virginia, that is, in thinking that numbers only ought to determine the weight of colonies. I think that property ought to be considered, and that it ought to be a compound of numbers and property that should determine the weight of the colonies. I think it cannot be now settled.

Mr. Rutledge. We have no legal authority; and obedience to our determinations will only follow the reasonableness, the apparent utility and necessity of the measures we adopt. We have no coercive or legislative authority. Our constituents are bound only in honor to observe our determinations.

Governor Ward. There are a great number of counties, in Virginia, very unequal in point of wealth and numbers, yet each has a right to send two members.

Mr. Lee. But one reason, which prevails with me, and that is, that we are not at this time provided with proper materials. I am afraid we are not.

Mr. Gadsden. I can't see any way of voting but by colonies.

Colonel Bland. I agree with the gentleman (ego) who spoke near me, that we are not at present provided with materials to ascertain the importance of each colony. The question is, whether the rights and liberties of America shall be contended for, or given up to arbitrary powers.

Mr. Pendleton. If the committee should find themselves unable to ascertain the weight of the colonies, by their numbers and property, they will report this, and this will lay the foundation for the Congress to take some other steps to procure evidence of numbers and property at some future time.

Mr. Henry. I agree that authentic accounts cannot be had, if by authenticity is meant attestations of officers of the Crown. I go upon the supposition that government is at an end. All distinctions are thrown down. All America is thrown into one mass. We must aim at the minutiæ of rectitude.

Mr. Jay. Could I suppose that we came to frame an American Constitution, instead of endeavoring to correct the faults in an old one—I can't yet think that all government is at an end. The measure of arbitrary power is not full, and I think it must run over, before we undertake to frame a new Constitution. To the virtue, spirit, and abilities of Virginia, we owe much. I should always, therefore, from inclination as well as justice, be for giving Virginia its full weight. I am not clear that we ought not to be bound by a majority, though ever so small, but I only mentioned it as a matter of danger, worthy of consideration. . . .

7. Wednesday. Went to Congress again, heard Mr. Duché read prayers; the collect for the day, the 7th of the month, was most admirably adapted, though this was accidental, or rather providential. A prayer which he gave us of his own composition was as pertinent, as affectionate, as sublime, as devout, as I ever heard offered up to Heaven. He filled every bosom present. . . .

10. Saturday. Attended my duty upon the subcommittee. Dined at home. Dr. Morgan, Dr. Cox, Mr. Spence, and several other gentlemen, Major Sullivan and Colonel Folsom, dined with us upon salt

fish.  Rambled in the evening with Jo Reed, and fell
into Mr. Sprout's meeting, where we heard Mr. Spence
preach.  Mr. Reed returned with Mr. Adams and me
to our lodgings, and a very sociable, agreeable, and
communicative evening we had.  He says we never
were guilty of a more masterly stroke of policy, than
in moving that Mr. Duché might read prayers; it has
had a very good effect, &c.  He says the sentiments
of people here are growing more and more favorable
every day.

11. Sunday.  There is such a quick and constant
succession of new scenes, characters, persons, and
events, turning up before me, that I can't keep any
regular account. . . .

12. Monday. . . . dined with Mr. Dickinson at
his seat at Fair Hill. . . . Mr. Dickinson has a fine
seat, a beautiful prospect of the city, the river, and
the country, fine gardens, and a very grand library.
. . . Mr. Dickinson is a very modest man, and very
ingenious as well as agreeable; he has an excellent
heart, and the cause of his country lies near it.  He is
full and clear for allowing to Parliament the regulation of trade, upon principles of necessity, and the
mutual interest of both countries.

13. Tuesday.  Attended my duty all day on the
sub-committee.  Agreed on a report.

14. Wednesday.  Visited Mr. Gadsden, Mr. Deane,
Colonel Dyer, &c., at their lodgings.  Gadsden is violent against allowing to Parliament any power of regulating trade, or allowing that they have anything to

do with us. "Power of regulating trade," he says, "is power of ruining us; as bad as acknowledging them a supreme legislative in all cases whatsoever; a right of regulating trade is a right of legislation, and a right of legislation in one case is a right in all; this I deny." Attended the Congress and committee all the forenoon; dined with Dr. Cox. . . . A mighty feast again; nothing less than the very best of Claret, Madeira, and Burgundy; melons, fine beyond description, and pears and peaches as excellent. This day Mr. Chase introduced to us a Mr. Carroll, of Annapolis, a very sensible gentleman, a Roman Catholic, and of the first fortune in America. His income is ten thousand pounds sterling a year now, will be fourteen in two or three years, they say; besides, his father has a vast estate which will be his after his father. . . .

17. Saturday. This was one of the happiest days of my life. In Congress we had generous, noble sentiments, and manly eloquence. This day convinced me that America will support the Massachusetts or perish with her. . . .

28. Wednesday. Dined with Mr. R. Penn; a magnificent house, and a most splendid feast, and a very large company. Mr. Dickinson and General Lee were there, and Mr. Moylan, besides a great number of the delegates. Spent the evening at home, with Colonel Lee, Colonel Washington, and Dr. Shippen, who came in to consult with us. . . .

[Oct] 10. Monday. The deliberations of the Congress are spun out to an immeasurable length. There is so much wit, sense, learning, acuteness, subtlety, eloquence, &c. among fifty gentlemen, each of whom has been habituated to lead and guide in his own province, that an immensity of time is spent unnecessarily. Johnson of Maryland has a clear and a cool head, an extensive knowledge of trade as well as law. He is a deliberating man, but not a shining orator; his passions and imagination don't appear enough for an orator; his reason and penetration appear, but not his rhetoric. Galloway, Duane, and Johnson are sensible and learned, but cold speakers. Lee, Henry, and Hooper, are the orators; Paca is a deliberator too; Chase speaks warmly; Mifflin is a sprightly and spirited speaker; John Rutledge don't exceed in learning or oratory, though he is a rapid speaker; young Edward Rutledge is young and zealous, a little unsteady and injudicious, but very unnatural and affected as a speaker; Dyer and Sherman speak often and long, but very heavily and clumsily. . . .

20. Thursday. Dined with the whole Congress, at the city tavern, at the invitation of the House of Representatives of the province of Pennsylvania. The whole House dined with us, making near one hundred guests in the whole; a most elegant entertainment. A sentiment was given: "May the sword of the parent never be stained with the blood of her children." Two or three broad-brims over against me at table; one of them said, this is not a toast, but a prayer; come, let us join in it. And they took their glasses accordingly. . . .

24. Monday.  In Congress, nibbling and quibbling as usual.  There is no greater mortification than to sit with half a dozen wits, deliberating upon a petition, address, or memorial.  These great wits, these subtle critics, these refined geniuses, these learned lawyers, these wise statesmen, are so fond of showing their parts and powers, as to make their consultations very tedious.  Young Ned Rutledge is a perfect Bob-o-Lincoln,—a swallow, a sparrow, a peacock; excessively vain, excessively weak, and excessively variable and unsteady; jejune, inane, and puerile.  Mr. Dickinson is very modest, delicate, and timid.  Spent the evening at home.  Colonel Dyer, Judge Sherman, and Colonel Floyd came in, and spent the evening with Mr. Adams and me.  Mr. Mifflin and General Lee came in.  Lee's head is running upon his new plan of a battalion. . . .

26. Wednesday.  Dined at home.  This day the Congress finished.  Spent the evening together at the city tavern; all the Congress, and several gentleman of the town. . . .

28. Friday.  Took our departure, in a very great rain, from the happy, the peaceful, the elegant, the hospitable, and polite city of Philadelphia.  It is not very likely that I shall ever see this part of the world again, but I shall ever retain a most grateful, pleasing sense of the many civilities I have received in it, and shall think myself happy to have an opportunity of returning them.

# "GIVE ME LIBERTY OR GIVE ME DEATH"

*Patrick Henry's Famous Virginia Convention Speech*

*HAVING utterly failed in farming and in trade, Patrick Henry, whose famous speech against British tyranny was made in 1775, studied law for a month in 1760 and had the boldness to ask for license to practice. It was granted to him, at the age of twenty-four, on condition that he would extend his studies before undertaking to practice.*

*Three years later Henry leapt into prominence by arguing a celebrated case, known as the "Parson's Cause," so brilliantly that the court-room audience bore him in triumph on their shoulders. Thereafter clients were plentiful.*

*This "liberty or death" exhortation was made shortly after he had served as a delegate to the first Continental Congress. His resolutions to organize the Virginia militia and put the colony in an attitude of defense were adopted unanimously after its delivery. Henry declined a United States Senatorship, declined to be Secretary of State under Washington, nor would he accept the Chief Justiceship of the U. S. Supreme Court.*

MR. PRESIDENT: It is natural to man to indulge in the illusions of hope. We are apt to shut our eyes against a painful truth—and listen to the song of that siren, till she transforms us into beasts. Is this the part of wise men, engaged in a great and arduous struggle for liberty? Are we disposed to be of the number of those, who having eyes, see not, and having ears, hear not, the things which so nearly concern their temporal salvation? For my part, whatever anguish of spirit it may cost, I am willing to know the whole truth; to know the worst, and to provide for it.

I have but one lamp by which my feet are guided; and that is the lamp of experience. I know of no way of judging of the future but by the past. And judging by the past, I wish to know what there has been in the conduct of the British ministry for the last ten years, to justify those hopes with which gentlemen have been pleased to solace themselves and the house? Is it that insidious smile with which our petition has been lately received? Trust it not, sir; it will prove a snare to your feet. Suffer not yourselves to be betrayed with a kiss. Ask yourselves how this gracious reception of our petition comports with those warlike preparations which cover our waters and darken our land. Are fleets and armies necessary to a work of love and reconciliation? Have we shown ourselves so unwilling to be reconciled that force must be called in to win back our love? Let us not deceive ourselves, sir. These are the implements of war and subjugation—the last arguments to which kings resort. I ask gentlemen, sir, what means this martial array, if its purpose be not to force us to submission? Can gentlemen assign any other possible motive for it? Has Great Britain any enemy in this quarter of the world, to call for all this accumulation of navies and armies? No, sir, she has none. They are meant for us: they can be meant for no other. They are sent over to bind and rivet upon us those chains which the British ministry have been so long forging. And what have we to oppose to them? Shall we try argument? Sir, we have been trying that for the last ten years. Have we anything new to offer upon the subject? Nothing. We have held the subject up in every light of which it is capable; but it has been all in vain. Shall we resort to entreaty and humble supplication? What terms shall we find which have not been already exhausted? Let us not, I beseech you, sir, deceive ourselves longer.

Sir, we have done everything that could be done to avert the storm which is now coming on. We have petitioned—we have remonstrated—we have supplicated—we have prostrated ourselves before the throne, and have implored its interposition to arrest the tyrannical hands of the ministry and parliament. Our petitions have been slighted; our remonstrances have produced additional violence and insult; our supplications have been disregarded; and we have been spurned, with contempt, from the foot of the throne. In vain, after these things, may we indulge the fond hope of peace and reconciliation. There is no longer any room for hope. If we wish to be free— if we mean to preserve inviolate those inestimable privileges for which we have been so long contending —if we mean not basely to abandon the noble struggle in which we have been so long engaged, and which we have pledged ourselves never to abandon until the glorious object of our contest shall be obtained—we must fight!—I repeat it, sir, we must fight!! An appeal to arms and to the God of Hosts, is all that is left us!

They tell us, sir, that we are weak—unable to cope with so formidable an adversary. But when shall we be stronger? Will it be the next week or the next year? Will it be when we are totally disarmed, and when a British guard shall be stationed in every house? Shall we gather strength by irresolution and inaction? Shall we acquire the means of effectual resistance by lying supinely on our backs, and hugging the delusive phantom of hope, until our enemies shall have bound us hand and foot? Sir, we are not weak, if we make a proper use of those means which the God of nature has placed in our power. Three millions of people, armed in the holy cause of liberty, and in such a country as that which we possess, are invincible by any force which our enemy can send against us. Besides, sir, we shall not fight our battles alone. There is a just God who presides over the destinies of nations; and who will raise up friends to fight our battles for us. The battle, sir, is not to the strong alone; it is to the vigilant, the active, the brave. Besides, sir, we have no election. If we were base enough to desire it, it is now too late to retire from the contest. There is no retreat but in submission and slavery! Our chains are forged. Their clanking may be heard on the plains of Boston! The war is inevitable—and let it come!! I repeat it, sir, let it come!!!

It is in vain, sir, to extenuate the matter. Gentlemen may cry, peace, peace—but there is no peace. The war is actually begun! The next gale that sweeps from the north will bring to our ears the clash of resounding arms! Our brethren are already in the field! Why stand we here idle? What is it that gentlemen wish? What would they have? Is life so dear, or peace so sweet, as to be purchased at the price of chains and slavery? Forbid it, Almighty God!—I know not what course others may take; but as for me, give me liberty or give me death!

# THE BATTLE OF LEXINGTON

*A Contemporary Account*

*SIX days after the first armed clash of the Revolutionary War occurred at Lexington, Mass., April 19, 1775, the accompanying report appeared in the Salem Gazette. This engagement, together with the contemporaneous one at Concord, was the turning-point between the period of protest and that of resistance in the colonies.*

*The objective of the British troops was the destruction of military stores at Concord, and also the seizure of John Hancock and Samuel Adams, residing at Lexington. Shortly after sunrise on the day of the battle, and after Paul Revere had spread the alarm, "The regulars are coming," Adams observed prophetically to Hancock, "What a glorious day!"*

LAST Wednesday the 19th of April, the troops of His Britannic Majesty commenced hostilities upon the people of this province, attended with circumstances of cruelty, not less brutal than what our venerable ancestors received from the vilest savages of the wilderness. The particulars relative to this interesting event, by which we are involved in all the horrors of a civil war, we have endeavored to collect as well as the present confused state of affairs will admit.

On Tuesday evening a detachment from the army, consisting, it is said, of eight or nine hundred men, commanded by Lieutenant Colonel Smith, embarked at the bottom of the Common in Boston, on board a number of boats, and landed at Phipps's farm, a little way up Charles River, from whence they proceeded with silence and expedition on their way to Concord, about eighteen miles from Boston. The people were soon alarmed, and began to assemble in several towns, before daylight, in order to watch the motion of the troops. At Lexington, six miles below Concord, a company of militia, of about one hundred men, mustered near the Meeting House; the troops came in sight of them just before sunrise; and running within a few rods of them, the commanding officer accosted the militia in words to this effect: "Disperse, you rebels—damn you, throw down your arms and disperse"; upon which the troops huzzaed, and immediately one or two officers discharged their pistols, which were instantaneously followed by the firing of four or five of the soldiers, and then there seemed to be a general discharge from the whole body: eight of our men were killed, and nine wounded. In a few minutes after this action the enemy renewed their march for Concord.

# THE BATTLE OF CONCORD

### By the Reverend William Emerson

*AN interesting feature of this account of the Lexington-Concord battle is that it was written by the grandfather of Ralph Waldo Emerson, who wrote the famous hymn sung at the completion of the Concord monument and referring to the "embattl'd farmers" who "fired the shot heard round the world."*

*At the time of the historic engagement, the Reverend William Emerson had a pastorate at Concord, Massachusetts, which is a short distance from Lexington and some eighteen miles from Boston. He became a chaplain in the Continental Army, and lost his life in the Ethan Allen expedition against Ticonderoga.*

*This article is printed in Whitney's "Literature of the Nineteenth of April," consisting of contemporaneous accounts of the initial battles of the Revolutionary War.*

THIS morning between one and two o'clock we were alarmed by the ringing of the bell —and upon examination found that the troops, to the number of 800, had stolen their march from Boston in boats and barges from the bottom of the Common over to a point in Cambridge near to Inman's farm, and were at Lexington Meeting House, half an hour before sunrise, where they had fired upon a body of our men, and (as we afterward heard) had killed several. This intelligence was brought us at first by Doctor Samuel Prescott, who narrowly escaped the guard that was sent before on horses, purposely to prevent all posts and messengers from giving us timely information. He, by the help of a very fleet horse, crossing several walls and fences, arrived at Concord at the time above mentioned.

When several posts were immediately dispatched, that returning confirmed the account of the Regulars' arrival at Lexington, and that they were on their way to Concord. Upon this a number of our Minute Men belonging to this town and Acton and Lincoln, with several others that were in readiness, marched out to meet them. While the alarm company were preparing to receive them in the town, Captain Minot, who commanded them, thought it proper to take possession of the hill above the Meeting House as the most advantageous situation.

No sooner had we gained it than we were met by the companies that were sent out to meet the troops, who informed us that they were just upon us, and that we must retreat, as their number was more than treble ours. We then retreated from the hill near the Liberty Pole and took a new post back of the town, upon a rising eminence, where we formed into two battalions, and awaited the arrival of the enemy.

Scarcely had we formed, before we saw the British troops, at the distance of a quarter of a mile, glittering in arms, advancing towards us with the greatest celerity. Some were for making a stand, notwithstanding the superiority of their number, but others more prudent thought best to retreat till our strength should be equal to the enemy's by recruits from neighboring towns that were continually coming to our assistance. Accordingly we retreated over the bridge when the troops came into the town, set fire to several carriages for the artillery, destroyed 60 barrels

of flour, rifled several houses, took possession of the
Town House, destroyed 500 pounds of balls, set a
guard of 100 men at the North Bridge and sent up a
party to the house of Colonel Barrett, where they
were in expectation of finding a quantity of warlike
stores; but these were happily secured just before
their arrival, by transportation into the woods and
other by-places.

In the meantime, the guard set by the enemy to
secure the pass at the North Bridge, were alarmed by
the approach of our people, who had retreated as mentioned before, and were now advancing, with special
orders not to fire upon the troops, unless fired upon.
These orders were so punctually observed that we received the fire of the enemy in three several and separate discharges of their pieces, before it was returned
by our commanding officer; the firing then soon became general for several minutes, in which skirmish
two were killed on each side, and several of the enemy
wounded. It may be observed by the way that we
were the more cautious to prevent beginning a rupture with the King's troops, as we were then uncertain
what had happened at Lexington, and knew [not]
that they had begun the quarrel there by first firing
upon our people and killing 8 men upon the spot.

The three companies of troops soon quitted their
post at the bridge, and retreated in greatest discord
and confusion to the main body, who were soon upon
the march to meet them. For half an hour the enemy
by their marches and counter-marches discovered

great fickleness and inconstancy of mind, sometimes advancing, sometimes returning to their former posts, till at length they quitted the town, and retreated by the way they came.   In the meantime a party of our men (150) took the back way through the great fields into the east quarter and had placed themselves to advantage, laying in ambush, behind walls, fences and buildings, ready to fire upon the enemy on their retreat.

# WASHINGTON APPOINTED COMMANDER-IN-CHIEF

*His Speech of Acceptance*

*CHARACTERISTICALLY plainspoken and sparing of words was Washington in accepting command of the Continental Army, tendered him in June, 1775, by the Continental Congress. His nomination was made by Thomas Johnson of Maryland, and was warmly seconded by John Adams.*

*To fill the post he was beyond question the best qualified man in the colonies. Not only was he competent in military affairs and skilled by precept and experience in the art of war, but his extensive knowledge of the geographical character of the country, and his familiarity with the characteristics and qualifications of the royal army, made him certainly the most dangerous antagonist, as a commanding officer, that the British could have had.*

MR. PRESIDENT: Though I am truly sensible of the high honor done me, in this appointment, yet I feel great distress, from a consciousness that my abilities and military experience may not be equal to the extensive and important trust. However, as the Congress desire it, I will enter upon the momentous duty, and exert every power I possess in their service, and for the support of the glorious cause. I beg they will accept my most cordial thanks for this distinguished testimony of their approbation.

But, lest some unlucky event should happen, unfavorable to my reputation, I beg it may be remembered by every gentleman in the room, that I, this day, declare with the utmost sincerity, I do not think myself equal to the command I am honored with.

As to pay, Sir, I beg leave to assure the Congress, that, as no pecuniary consideration could have tempted me to accept this arduous employment, at the expense of my domestic ease and happiness, I do not wish to make any profit from it.   I will keep an exact account of my expenses.   Those, I doubt not, they will discharge, and that is all I desire.

# FAREWELL TO MRS. WASHINGTON

*GEORGE WASHINGTON met Martha Dandridge, the widow of Daniel Parker Custis, in the Spring of 1758. At their second meeting he made a proposal of marriage which she accepted and on January 6th of the following year they were married.*

*It is said that after General Washington's death, Martha Washington shut herself up in her room at Mount Vernon and spent her time sitting before the window which looked out on his tomb. Shortly before her death Martha Washington destroyed all of the personal letters from her husband that she had in her possession. The letter given here, dated Philadelphia, June 18, 1775, is one of the few that has come down to us.*

"MY DEAREST: I am now set down to write to you on a subject, which fills me with inexpressible concern, and this concern is greatly aggravated and increased, when I reflect upon the uneasiness I know it will give you. It has been determined in Congress, that the whole army raised for the defense of the American cause shall be put under my care, and that it is necessary for me to proceed immediately to Boston to take upon me the command of it.

"You may believe me, my dear Patsy, when I assure you, in the most solemn manner, that, so far from seeking this appointment, I have used every endeavor in my power to avoid it, not only from my unwillingness to part with you and the family, but from a consciousness of its being a trust too great for my capacity, and that I should enjoy more real happiness in one month with you at home, than I have the most distant prospect of finding abroad, if my stay were to be seven times seven years. But as it has been a kind of destiny, that has thrown me upon this service, I shall hope that my undertaking it is designed to answer some good purpose. You might, and I suppose did perceive, from the tenor of my letters, that I was apprehensive I could not avoid this appointment, as I did not pretend to intimate when I should return. That was the case. It was utterly out of my power to refuse this appointment, without exposing my character to such censures, as would have reflected dishonor upon myself, and given pain to my friends. This, I am sure, could not, and ought not, to be pleasing to you, and must have lessened me considerably in my own esteem. I shall rely, therefore, confidently on that Providence, which has heretofore preserved and been bountiful to me, not doubting but that I shall return safe to you in the fall. I shall feel no pain from the toil or the danger of the campaign; my unhappiness will flow from the uneasiness I know you will feel from being left alone. I therefore beg, that you will summon your whole fortitude, and pass your time as agreeably as possible. Nothing will give me so much sincere satisfaction as to hear this, and to hear it from your own pen. My earnest and ardent desire is, that you would pursue any plan that is most likely to produce content, and a tolerable degree of tranquillity; as it must add greatly to my uneasy feelings to hear, that you are dissatisfied or complaining at what I really could not avoid.

As life is always uncertain, and common prudence dictates to every man the necessity of settling his temporal concerns, while it is in his power, and while the mind is calm and undisturbed, I have, since I came to this place (for I had not time to do it before I left home) got Colonel Pendleton to draft a will for me, by the directions I gave him, which will I now enclose. The provision made for you in case of my death will, I hope, be agreeable.

I shall add nothing more, as I have several letters to write, but to desire that you will remember me to your friends, and to assure you that I am, with the most unfeigned regard, my dear Patsy, your affectionate, &c."

# WASHINGTON AT CAMBRIDGE

*Washington's Letter to the President of Congress, on His Arrival at Cambridge to Take Command of the Army*

*F*OLLOWING his appointment as Commander-in-Chief of the American army, General Washington arrived in Cambridge, Mass., on July 2, 1775, after journeying eleven days from Philadelphia, and on the next day, under the famous elm which marked the spot for nearly a century and a half, he took formal command, succeeding General Artemas Ward. Eight days later he addressed this communication to Congress.

The event took place in Cambridge because it had been decided to press the siege of Boston, and Washington was resolved to drive the British out, as his first task. Meanwhile the Massachusetts Provincial Congress appointed a Committee of Safety to confer with Washington about a suitable residence for himself and General Lee, who had accompanied him, and a mansion subsequently known as the "Craigie house," belonging to a refugee loyalist, was immediately prepared for their reception.

*S*IR, I arrived safe at this place on the 3d inst., after a journey attended with a good deal of fatigue, and retarded by necessary attentions to the successive civilities which accompanied me in my whole route. Upon my arrival, I immediately visited the several posts occupied by our troops, and as soon as the weather permitted, reconnoitred those of the enemy. I found the latter strongly entrenched on Bunker's Hill about a mile from Charlestown, and advanced about half a mile from the place of the last action, with their sentries extended about 150 yards on this side of the narrowest part of the neck leading from this place to Charlestown. . . .

The bulk of their army commanded by General Howe, lays on Bunker's Hill, and the remainder on Roxbury Neck, except the Light Horse, and a few men in the town of Boston.  On our side we have thrown up entrenchments on Winter and Prospect Hills, the enemy's camp in full view at the distance of little more than a mile.  Such intermediate points, as would admit a landing, I have since my arrival taken care to strengthen, down to Sewall's farm, where a strong entrenchment has been thrown up. . . .

My earnest wishes to comply with the instructions of the Congress in making an early and complete return of the state of the army, has led into an involuntary delay in addressing you, which has given me much concern.  Having given orders for this purpose immediately on my arrival, and unapprized of the imperfect obedience which had been paid to those of the like nature from General Ward, I was led from day to day to expect they would come in, and therefore detained the messenger.  They are not now so complete as I could wish, but much allowance is to be made for inexperience in forms, and a liberty which has been taken (not given) on this subject. These reasons I flatter myself will no longer exist, and of consequence more regularity and exactness in future prevail. . . .

We labor under great disadvantages for want of tents, for though they have been helped out by a collection of now useless sails from the seaport towns, the number is yet far short of our necessities.  The colleges and houses of this town are necessarily occupied by the troops, which affords another reason for keeping our present situation. But I most sincerely wish the whole army was properly provided to take the field, as I am well assured, that besides greater expedition and activity in case of alarm, it would highly conduce to health and discipline. As materials are not to be had here, I would beg leave to recommend the procuring a further supply from Philadelphia as soon as possible. . . .

I find myself already much embarrassed for want of a military chest; these embarrassments will increase every day: I must therefore request that money may be forwarded as soon as possible. The want of this most necessary article, will I fear produce great inconveniences if not prevented by an early attention. I find the army in general, and the troops raised in Massachusetts in particular, very deficient in necessary clothing. Upon inquiry there appears no probability of obtaining any supplies in this quarter. And the best consideration of this matter I am able to form, I am of opinion that a number of hunting shirts not less than 10,000, would in a great degree remove this difficulty in the cheapest and quickest manner. I know nothing in a speculative view more trivial, yet if put in practice would have a happier tendency to unite the men, and abolish those provincial distinctions which lead to jealousy and dissatisfaction. In a former part of this letter I mentioned the want of engineers; I can hardly express the disappointment

I have experienced on this subject. The skill of those we have, being very imperfect and confined to the mere manual exercise of cannon: Whereas—the war in which we are engaged requires a knowledge comprehending the duties of the field and fortifications. If any persons thus qualified are to be found in the southern colonies, it would be of great public service to forward them with all expedition. Upon the article of ammunition I must reëcho the former complaints on this subject: We are so exceedingly destitute, that our artillery will be of little use without a supply both large and seasonable: What we have must be reserved for the small arms, and that managed with the utmost frugality.

I am sorry to observe that the appointments of the general officers in the province of Massachusetts Bay have by no means corresponded with the judgment and wishes of either the civil or military. The great dissatisfaction expressed on this subject and the apparent danger of throwing the army into the utmost disorder, together with the strong representations of the provincial Congress, have induced me to retain the commissions in my hands until the pleasure of the Congress should be farther known, (except General Putnam's which was given the day I came into camp and before I was apprized of these uneasinesses). In such a step I must beg the Congress will do me the justice I believe, that I have been, actuated solely by a regard to the public good. I have not, nor could have any private attachments; every gentleman in appointment, was an entire stranger to me but from character. I must therefore rely upon the candor of the Congress for their favorable construction of my conduct in this particular. General Spencer was so much disgusted at the preference given to General Putnam that he left the army without visiting me, or making known his intentions in any respect. General Pomroy had also retired before my arrival, occasioned (as is said) by some disappointment from the Provincial Congress. General Thomas is much esteemed and earnestly desired to continue in the service; and as far as my opportunities have enabled me to judge I must join in the general opinion that he is an able good officer and his resignation would be a public loss. The postponing him to Pomroy and Heath whom he has commanded would make his continuance very difficult and probably operate on his mind, as the like circumstance has done on that of Spencer. . . .

The deficiency of numbers, discipline and stores can only lead to this conclusion, that their spirit has exceeded their strength. But at the same time I would humbly submit to the consideration of the Congress, the propriety of making some further provision of men from the other colonies. If these regiments should be completed to their establishment, the dismission of those unfit for duty on account of their age and character would occasion a considerable reduction, and at all events they have been enlisted upon such terms, that they may be disbanded when other troops arrive. But should my apprehensions be realized, and the regiments here not filled up, the public cause would suffer by an absolute dependence upon so doubtful an event, unless some provision is made against such a disappointment.

It requires no military skill to judge of the difficulty of introducing proper discipline and subordination into an army while we have the enemy in view, and are in daily expectation of an attack, but it is of so much importance that every effort will be made which time and circumstance will admit. In the meantime I have a sincere pleasure in observing that there are materials for a good army, a great number of able-bodied men, active zealous in the cause and of un-questionable courage. . . .

# THE BATTLE OF BUNKER HILL

*By a Leader of the Provincial Forces*

*THIS letter, dated June 26, 1775—ten days after the battle—was written by a colonial participant to a friend in England and was printed a month or so later in the London Morning Post and Daily Advertiser. It was recently found in the files of that paper, and is included in a volume of "Letters on the American Revolution," edited by Margaret Wheeler Willard (Houghton-Mifflin.)*

*The importance of the Battle of Bunker (or rather, Breed's) Hill in revolutionizing public and private opinion in the colonies is evidenced by other letters. One written from New York before the news of Bunker Hill had arrived states, "It is a gross calumny to say that we are aiming at independency." In the reaction to that battle, however, the feeling against independence began to break down and in the following year crystallized into a national desire for freedom. A Quaker writes from Philadelphia, in 1776, that "the time is not far off when the colonies will set up an independent standard."*

STRICT orders having been given that no letter shall be received on board the men-of-war from any of those who have the courage to appear in arms against the unconstitutional and oppressive measures of administration, and the late inflated proclamation having pronounced such severe penalties against those who shall correspond with men thus acting in defence of all those great and essential privileges which our forefathers ever held so dear, it becomes difficult for me to convey, or perhaps for you to receive any information from this side of the water, except from men retained in the pay of the administration, who have every inducement which profit and prejudice can inspire to misrepresent the truth. After the windy proclamation of the

12th, our troops became enraged because they were not led on to action. This learned proclamation was burned by the hands of the common hangman at Cambridge, Roxburgh, [Roxbury] and Deutester-wick [Dorchester]. Many went off in disgust that nothing was done; the different parishes sent them back; they stated the case of their desertion. Finding the zeal of the troops so great, and that notwithstand-ing the threatening of the proclamation, we were not likely to feel the effects of those who bear the sword so soon as was expected, it was resolved to force Gen-eral Gage to an action. With this in view it was de-termined to seize possession of the height on the peninsula of Charlestown, which General Gage had occupied before the 19th of April, and erect some bat-teries on Banhin-hill [Bunker-hill], to batter down the town and General Gage's camp on the Common and his entrenchment on Boston Neck (which is only about three fourths of a mile across). Four thousand men commanded by General Putnam, and led on by Dr. Warren, having prepared every thing for the operation as well as could be contrived or collected were stationed under a half unfinished breastwork and some palisadoes fixed in a hurry. When the enemy were landed, to the number of 2500, as we are since informed, being the light infantry and the grenadiers of the army with a complete train of artillery, howit-zers and field pieces, drawn by 200 sailors, and com-manded by the most gallant and experienced officers of the last war, they marched to engage 3000 provin-

cials, arrayed in red worsted caps and blue great coats,
with guns of different sizes, few of which had
bayonets, ill-served artillery, but of invincible courage! The fire from the ships and artillery of the
enemy was horrid and amazing; the first onset of the
soldiers was bold and fierce, but they were received
with equal courage; at length the 38th Regiment gave
way, and the rest recoiled. The King's troops were
commanded by General Howe, brother to that gallant
Lord Howe to whose memory the province of Massa-
chusett's Bay erected a statue. He marched with un-
daunted spirit at the head of his men; most of his
followers were killed round his own person. The
King's troops about this time got into much confusion and retreated, but were rallied by the re-
proaches of General Howe, and the activity of General Clinton who then joined the battle. The King's
troops again made their push against Charlestown,
which was then set on fire by them. Our right flank
being then uncovered, two floating batteries coming
in by the mill dam to take us in the rear, more troops
coming from Boston, and our ammunition being almost expended, General Putnam ordered the troops
on the left to retreat. The confusion was great for
twenty minutes, but in less than half an hour we fell
into complete order; the regulars were so mauled they
durst not pursue us 200 yards, but almost the last shot
they fired killed good Dr. Warren, who had dressed
himself like Lord Falkland, in his wedding suit, and
distinguished himself by unparalleled acts of bravery

during the whole action, but particularly in covering the retreat. He was a man of great courage, universal learning and much humanity. It may well be said he is the greatest loss we have sustained. General Putnam, at the age of 60, was as active as the youngest officer in the field. We have lost 104 killed, and 306 wounded; a Lieutenant Colonel and 30 men are prisoners, and we anxiously wait their fate. We lost before the action began 18 men by the fire of the ships and the battery from Boston, burying them before the assault. The number of the King's troops killed and wounded are three times our loss. A sailor belonging to one of the transports, who was busy with many of his companions in rifling the dead, and who has since deserted, assured me the ground was covered with officers. The cannonading was dreadful. The King's troops began firing at a great distance, being scarce of ammunition deferred our fire. It was impossible to send troops from Roxburgh, because we expected an attack there, or at Dorchester neck. I am well informed many of the old English officers are since dead.

When General Gage had the inhabitants of Boston pent up in the town, not less than five hundred marksmen at different times went out in dung carts covered with dirt to join the army, and carried off 10 or 12,000 cartridges of ammunition by the same means, without being discovered. On the 19th two beautiful young men, between 25 and 30 years of age, devoted themselves to death. They marched within General Gage's sentinels on the neck; a sergeant and six men were sent to receive them, thinking they came to lay down their arms; when they approached they told the troops "the King's ministers had treated them as slaves, the King's officers had reported them as cowards, that they came to show the falsity of both reports and the weakness of the proclamation, by sealing with their blood their firm belief in the justice of their cause, upon which they were ready immediately to appear before the presence of God." Here they fired and killed two of the enemy; they were immediately fired at again, and one was instantly killed and the other desperately wounded, but he told the King's troops he did not desire to live, and demanded they should kill him also, which was soon complied with. I do declare as a man of veracity, under all the hardships our people have undergone, I have not heard one complain of his personal suffering. They bewail each others' misfortunes; they complain bitterly of the cruelties of the English administration; they lament the separation of the Empire which is likely to take place, but of their own particular sufferings no man murmurs or complains. Not a soldier dies of his wounds who does not believe he goes directly to heaven, notwithstanding all the anathemas of the general proclamation. If this business continues till November you will have an account of ships and troops. If we could have imagined the Parliament of England could have been so infatuated as appears by their proceedings of last session of Parliament, we should certainly have destroyed the small few then in this province.

# PAUL REVERE TELLS OF HIS MIDNIGHT RIDE

*Deposition of 1775*

*PAUL REVERE* really lived and his midnight ride, celebrated by Longfellow, actually took place. Longfellow obtained the material for his famous poem from a letter which Revere wrote about twenty-two years after the events it describes; and this letter was based on a deposition, reprinted here from the original manuscript, which Revere made shortly after the ride.

Instead of being merely a clever despatch rider, however, Paul Revere was one of the most versatile men of his time— patriot, politician and soldier, goldsmith, artist and engraver, inventor, bell founder, dentist, industrial pioneer. As a goldsmith he was accustomed to deliver his wares, on horseback, to his country customers, thus becoming an expert horseman. In 1774 he had ridden from Boston to Philadelphia scattering the hated Boston Port Act, which provoked the first Continental Congress.

The concluding event described in this deposition is the Battle of Lexington that Revere witnessed.

I, PAUL REVERE, of Boston, in the colony of the Massachusetts Bay in New England; of lawful age, do testify and say; that I was sent for by Dr. Joseph Warren, of said Boston, on the evening of the 18th of April, about 10 o'clock; when he desired me, "to go to Lexington, and inform Mr. Samuel Adams, and the Hon. John Hancock Esq. that there was a number of soldiers, composed of light troops, and grenadiers, marching to the bottom of the common, where was a number of boats to receive them; it was supposed, that they were going to Lexington, by the way of Cambridge River, to take them, or go to Concord, to destroy the colony stores."

I proceeded immediately, and was put across Charles River and landed near Charlestown Battery; went in town, and there got a horse. While in Charlestown, I was informed by Richard Devens Esq. that he met that evening, after sunset, nine officers of the ministerial army [British regulars], mounted on good horses, and armed, going towards Concord.

I set off, it was then about 11 o'clock, the moon shone bright. I had got almost over Charlestown Common, towards Cambridge, when I saw two officers on horse-back, standing under the shade of a tree, in a narrow part of the road. I was near enough to see their holsters and cockades. One of them started his horse towards me, the other up the road, as I supposed, to head me, should I escape the first. I turned my horses short about, and rode upon a full gallop for Mistick Road, he followed me about 300 yards, and finding he could not catch me, returned. I proceeded to Lexington, through Mistick, and alarmed Mr. Adams and Col. Hancock.

After I had been there about half an hour Mr. Daws arrived, who came from Boston, over the Neck.

We set off for Concord, and were overtaken by a young gentleman named Prescot, who belonged to Concord, and was going home. When we had got about half way from Lexington to Concord, the other two stopped at a house to awake the man, I kept along. When I had got about 200 yards ahead of them, I saw two officers as before. I called to my company to come up, saying here was two of them,

(for I had told them what Mr. Devens told me, and of my being stopped).    In an instant I saw four of them, who rode up to me with their pistols in their hands, said "G—d d—n you, stop.    If you go an inch further, you are a dead man."    Immediately Mr. Prescot came up.    We attempted to get through them, but they kept before us, and swore if we did not turn in to that pasture, they would blow our brains out, (they had placed themselves opposite to a pair of bars, and had taken the bars down).    They forced us in.    When we had got in, Mr. Prescot said "Put on!"    He took to the left, I to the right towards a wood at the bottom of the pasture, intending, when I gained that, to jump my horse and run afoot.    Just as I reached it, out started six officers, seized my bridle, put their pistols to my breast, ordered me to dismount, which I did. One of them, who appeared to have the command there, and much of a gentleman, asked me where I came from; I told him.    He asked what time I left it.    I told him, he seemed surprised, said "Sir, may I crave your name?"    I answered "My name is Revere."    "What" said he, "Paul Revere"?    I answered "Yes."    The others abused much; but he told me not to be afraid, no one should hurt me.    I told him they would miss their aim.    He said they should not, they were only waiting for some deserters they expected down the road.    I told him I knew better, I knew what they were after; that I had alarmed the country all the way up, that their boats were caught aground, and I should have 500 men there soon.    One of them said they had 1500 coming; he seemed surprised and rode off into the road, and informed them who took me, they came down immediately on a full gallop. One of them (whom I since learned was Major Mitchel of the 5th Reg.) clapped his pistol to my head, and said he was going to ask me some questions, and if I did not tell the truth, he would blow my brains out. I told him I esteemed myself a man of truth, that he had stopped me on the highway, and made me a prisoner, I knew not by what right; I would tell him the truth; I was not afraid. He then asked me the same questions that the other did, and many more, but was more particular; I gave him much the same answers. He then ordered me to mount my horse, they first searched me for pistols. When I was mounted, the Major took the reins out of my hand, and said "By G—d Sir, you are not to ride with reins I assure you"; and gave them to an officer on my right, to lead me. He then ordered 4 men out of the bushes, and to mount their horses; they were country men which they had stopped who were going home; then ordered us to march. He said to me, "We are now going towards your friends, and if you attempt to run, or we are insulted, we will blow your brains out." When we had got into the road they formed a circle, and ordered the prisoners in the center, and to lead me in the front. We rode towards Lexington at a quick pace; they very often insulted me calling me rebel, etc., etc. After we had got about a mile, I was given to the sergeant to lead, he was ordered to take out his pistol, (he rode with a hanger,) and if I ran, to execute the major's sentence.

When we got within about half a mile of the Meeting House we heard a gun fired. The Major asked me what it was for, I told him to alarm the country; he ordered the four prisoners to dismount, they did, then one of the officers dismounted and cut the bridles and saddles off the horses, and drove them away, and told the men they might go about their business. I asked the Major to dismiss me, he said he would carry me, let the consequence be what it will. He then ordered us to march.

When we got within sight of the Meeting House, we heard a volley of guns fired, as I supposed at the tavern, as an alarm; the Major ordered us to halt, he asked me how far it was to Cambridge, and many more questions, which I answered. He then asked the sergeant, if his horse was tired, he said yes; he ordered him to take my horse. I dismounted, and the sergeant mounted my horse; they cut the bridle and saddle of the sergeant's horse, and rode off down the road. I then went to the house were I left Messrs. Adams and Hancock, and told them what had happened; their friends advised them to go out of the way; I went with them, about two miles across road.

After resting myself, I set off with another man to go back to the tavern, to inquire the news; when we got there, we were told the troops were within two miles. We went into the tavern to get a trunk of papers belonging to Col. Hancock. Before we left the house, I saw the ministerial troops from the chamber window. We made haste, and had to pass through our militia, who were on a green behind the Meeting House, to the number as I supposed, about 50 or 60, I went through them; as I passed I heard the commanding officer speak to his men to this purpose, "Let the troops pass by, and don't molest them, without they begin first." I had to go across road; but had not got half gunshot off, when the ministerial troops appeared in sight, behind the Meeting House. They made a short halt, when one gun was fired. I heard the report, turned my head, and saw the smoke in front of the troops. They immediately gave a great shout, ran a few paces, and then the whole fired. I could first distinguish irregular firing, which I supposed was the advance guard, and then platoons; at this time I could not see our militia, for they were covered from me by a house at the bottom of the street. And further saith not.

PAUL REVERE.

# THE DRAMATIC CAPTURE OF TICONDEROGA

*By Ethan Allen*

*COMING between the Battles of Lexington and Bunker Hill, the surprise and capture of Fort Ticonderoga, at the head of Lake George, on May 10, 1775, by Colonel Ethan Allen and a band of Green Mountain Boys, was the first complete victory scored by the colonists in the Revolutionary War. This account of it is taken from a "Narrative of Colonel Ethan Allen's Captivity," published in 1779. He was captured near Montreal four months after the Ticonderoga exploit while engaged on a secret mission to Canada.*

*The ease with which Ticonderoga was taken is partly explained by the fact that it was weakly garrisoned after the cession of Canada to Great Britain. In 1777 Burgoyne invested it and forced its evacuation by the Americans. Later the British were attacked in turn by General Lincoln, who released 100 American prisoners and took 293 of the English, but failed to recover the fort itself.*

EVER since I arrived at the state of manhood, and acquainted myself with the general history of mankind, I have felt a sincere passion for liberty. The history of nations doomed to perpetual slavery, in consequence of yielding up to tyrants their natural-born liberties, I read with a sort of philosophical horror; so that the first systematical and bloody attempt, at Lexington, to enslave America, thoroughly electrified my mind, and fully determined me to take part with my country. And, while I was wishing for an opportunity to signalize myself in its behalf, directions were privately sent to me from the then colony (now State) of Connecticut, to raise the Green Mountain Boys, and, if possible, with them to surprise and take the fortress of Ticonderoga.

This enterprise I cheerfully undertook; and, after first guarding all the several passes that led thither, to cut off all intelligence between the garrison and the country, made a forced march from Bennington, and arrived at the lake opposite to Ticonderoga, on the evening of the ninth day of May, 1775, with two hundred and thirty valiant Green Mountain Boys; and it was with the utmost difficulty that I procured boats to cross the lake. However, I landed eighty-three men near the garrison, and sent the boats back for the rear guard, commanded by Colonel Seth Warner; but the day began to dawn, and I found myself under necessity to attack the fort before the rear could cross the lake; and, as it was viewed hazardous, I harangued the officers and soldiers in the manner following:

"Friends and fellow-soldiers, You have, for a number of years past been a scourge and terror to arbitrary power. Your valor has been famed abroad, and acknowledged, as appears by the advice and orders to me, from the General Assembly of Connecticut, to surprise and take the garrison now before us. I now propose to advance before you, and, in person, conduct you through the wicket-gate; for we must this morning either quit our pretensions to valor, or possess ourselves of this fortress in a few minutes; and, inasmuch as it is a desperate attempt, which none but the bravest of men dare undertake, I do not urge it on any contrary to his will. You that will undertake voluntarily, poise your firelocks."

The men being, at this time, drawn up in three ranks, each poised his firelock. I ordered them to face to the right, and, at the head of the center-file, marched them immediately to the wicket-gate aforesaid, where I found a sentry posted, who instantly snapped his fusee at me; I ran immediately toward him, and he retreated through the covered way into the parade within the garrison, gave a halloo, and ran under a bomb-proof. My party, who followed me into the fort, I formed on the parade in such a manner as to face the two barracks which faced each other.

The garrison being asleep, except the sentries, we gave three huzzas which greatly surprised them. One of the sentries made a pass at one of my officers with a charged bayonet, and slightly wounded him. My first thought was to kill him with my sword; but, in an instant, I altered the design and fury of the blow to a slight cut on the side of the head, upon which he dropped his gun, and asked quarter, which I readily granted him, and demanded of him the place where the commanding officer kept. He showed me a pair of stairs in the front of a barrack, on the west part of the garrison, which led up to a second story in said barrack, to which I immediately repaired, and ordered the commander, Captain De la Place, to come forth instantly, or I would sacrifice the whole garrison; at which the Captain came immediately to the door, with his breeches in his hand. When I ordered him to deliver me the fort instantly, he asked me by what authority I demanded it. I answered him, "In the name of the great Jehovah, and the Continental Congress."

The authority of the Congress being very little known at that time, he began to speak again; but I interrupted him, and with my drawn sword over his head, again demanded an immediate surrender of the garrison; with which he then complied, and ordered his men to be forthwith paraded without arms, as he had given up the garrison. In the mean time some of my officers had given orders, and in consequence thereof, sundry of the barrack doors were beat down, and about one-third of the garrison imprisoned, which consisted of the said commander, a Lieutenant Feltham, a conductor of artillery, a gunner, two sergeants, and forty-four rank and file; about one hundred pieces of cannon, one thirteen-inch mortar, and a number of swivels. This surprise was carried into execution in the gray of the morning of the tenth of May, 1775. The sun seemed to rise that morning with a superior lustre; and Ticonderoga and its dependencies smiled to its conquerors, who tossed about the flowing bowl, and wished success to Congress, and the liberty and freedom of America.

# A CALL FOR INDEPENDENCE

## By Thomas Paine

*THOMAS PAINE'S "Common Sense," of which this is the appendix, was published anonymously six months before the drafting of the Declaration of Independence, which it advocated and inspired. Indeed, there might never have been any such revolutionary declaration had this pamphlet not been published and read throughout the colonies in the early months of 1776. It converted Washington, who pronounced it, "Sound logic and unanswerable reasoning," and its influence on Jefferson and Franklin was marked. John Adams, who had no love for Paine, once wrote to Jefferson, "History is to ascribe to Paine the Revolution," and Lafayette said repeatedly, "To me America without Paine is unthinkable."*

*Paine was the son of an English Quaker, a staymaker, and was living somewhat precariously in London in 1774 when Benjamin Franklin, attracted by his genius, persuaded him to emigrate to America, with letters of introduction to his friends.*

LEAVING the moral part to private reflection, I shall chiefly confine my further remarks to the following heads:

First, That it is the interest of America to be separated from Britain.

Secondly, Which is the easiest and most practicable plan, reconciliation or independence? with some occasional remarks.

In support of the first, I could, if I judged it proper, produce the opinion of some of the ablest and most experienced men on this continent; and whose sentiments, on that head, are not yet publicly known. It is in reality a self-evident position: For no nation, in a state of foreign dependence, limited in its commerce, and cramped and fettered in its legislative powers, can

151

ever arrive at any material eminence. America does not yet know what opulence is; and although the progress which she has made stands unparalleled in the history of other nations, it is but childhood, compared with what she would be capable of arriving at, had she, as she ought to have, the legislative powers in her own hands. England is, at this time, proudly coveting what would do her no good, were she to accomplish it; and the continent hesitating on a matter, which will be her final ruin if neglected. It is the commerce, and not the conquest of America, by which England is to be benefited, and that would in a great measure continue, were the countries as independent of each other as France and Spain; because in many articles, neither can go to a better market. But it is the independence of this country on Britain or any other, which is now the main and only object worthy of contention, and which, like all other truths discovered by necessity, will appear clearer and stronger every day.

First. Because it will come to that one time or other.

Secondly. Because the longer it is delayed, the harder it will be to accomplish.

I have frequently amused myself both in public and private companies, with silently remarking the specious errors of those who speak without reflecting. And among the many which I have heard, the following seems the most general, viz. that had this rupture happened forty or fifty years hence, instead of now, the Continent would have been more able to have shaken off the dependence. To which I reply, that our military ability at this time, arises from the experience gained in the late war, and which in forty or fifty years time, would have been totally extinct. . . .

Should affairs be patched up with Britain, and she to remain the governing and sovereign power of America, (which as matters are now circumstanced, is giving up the point entirely) we shall deprive ourselves of the very means of sinking the debt we have, or may contract. The value of the back lands, which some of the provinces are clandestinely deprived of, by the unjust extension of the limits of Canada, valued only at five pounds sterling per hundred acres, amount to upwards of twenty-five millions, Pennsylvania currency; and the quit-rents at one penny sterling per acre, to two millions yearly. . . .

I proceed now to the second head, viz. Which is the easiest and most practicable plan, Reconciliation or Independence; with some occasional remarks.

He who takes nature for his guide, is not easily beaten out of his argument, and on that ground, I answer generally, that independence being a single simple line, contained within ourselves; and reconciliation, a matter of exceedingly perplexed and complicated, and in which, a treacherous capricious court is to interfere, gives the answer without a doubt.

The present state of America is truly alarming to every man who is capable of reflection. Without law, without government, without any other mode of power than what is founded on, and granted by courtesy. Held together by an unexampled concurrence of sentiment, which, is nevertheless subject to change, and which, every secret enemy is endeavoring to dissolve. Our present condition is, legislation without law; wisdom without a plan; a Constitution without a name; and, what is strangely astonishing, perfect independence, contending for dependence. The instance is without a precedent; the case never existed before; and who can tell what may be the event? The property of no man is secure in the present unbraced system of things. The mind of the multitude is left at random, and seeing no fixed object before them, they pursue such as fancy or opinion starts. Nothing is criminal; there is no such thing as treason; wherefore, every one thinks himself at liberty to act as he pleases. The Tories would not have dared to assemble offensively, had they known that their lives, by that act, were forfeited to the laws of the State. A line of distinction should be drawn between English soldiers taken in battle, and inhabitants of America taken in arms. The first are prisoners, but the latter traitors. The one forfeits his liberty, the other his head. . . .

Put us, say some, upon the footing we were on in sixty-three. . . . To be on the footing of sixty-three, it is not sufficient, that the laws only be put on the same state, but that our circumstances, likewise be put on the same state; our burnt and destroyed towns repaired or built up, our private losses made good, our public debts (contracted for defense) discharged; otherwise we shall be millions worse than we were at that enviable period. Such a request, had it been complied with a year ago, would have won the heart and soul of the Continent, but now it is too late. "The Rubicon is passed."

Besides, the taking up arms, merely to enforce the repeal of a pecuniary law, seems as unwarrantable by the divine law, and as repugnant to human feelings, as the taking up arms to enforce the obedience thereto. The object, on either side, does not justify the means; for the lives of men are too valuable, to be cast away on such trifles. It is the violence which is done and threatened to our persons; the destruction of our property by an armed force; the invasion of our country by fire and sword, which conscientiously qualifies the use of arms: And the instant, in which such a mode of defense became necessary, all subjection to Britain ought to have ceased; and the independency of America, should have been considered, as dating its era from, and published, by the first musket that was fired against her. This line is a line of consistency; neither drawn by caprice, nor extended by ambition; but produced by a chain of events, of which the colonies were not the authors.

I shall conclude these remarks, with the following timely and well intended hint. We ought to reflect that there are three different ways, by which an independency may hereafter be effected; and that one of those three, will one day or other, be the fate of America, viz. By the legal voice of the people in Congress; by a military power; or by a mob. It may not always happen that our soldiers are citizens, and the multitude a body of reasonable men; virtue, as I have already remarked, is not hereditary, neither is it perpetual. Should an independency be brought about by the first of those means, we have every opportunity and every encouragement before us, to form the noblest purest constitution on the face of the earth. We have it in our power to begin the world over again. A situation, similar to the present, has not happened since the days of Noah until now. The birthday of a new world is at hand, and a race of men, perhaps as numerous as all Europe contains, are to receive their portion of freedom from the event of a few months. The reflection is awful and in this point of view, how trifling, how ridiculous, do the little paltry cavilings, of a few weak or interested men appear, when weighed against the business of a world. . . .

In short, independence is the only bond that can tie and keep us together. We shall then see our object, and our ears will be legally shut against the schemes of an intriguing, as well as a cruel enemy. We shall then too be on a proper footing to treat with Britain; for there is reason to conclude, that the pride of that court will be less hurt by treating with the American states for terms of peace, than with those she denominates "rebellious subjects," for terms of accommodation. It is our delaying it that encourages her to hope for conquest, and our backwardness tends only to prolong the war. As we have, without any good effect therefrom, withheld our trade to obtain a redress of our grievances, let us now try the alternative, by independently redressing them ourselves, and then offering to open the trade. The mercantile and reasonable part in England will be still with us; because, peace with trade, is preferable to war without it. And if this offer is not accepted, other courts may be applied to. On these grounds I rest the matter. And as no offer hath yet been made to refute the doctrine contained in the former editions of this pamphlet, it is a negative proof, that either the doctrine cannot be refuted, or, that the party in favor of it are too numerous to be opposed. Wherefore instead of gazing at each other with suspicious or doubtful curiosity, let each of us hold out to his neighbor the hearty hand of friendship, and unite in drawing a line, which, like an act of oblivion, shall bury in forgetfulness every former dissension. Let the names of Whig and Tory be extinct; and let none other be heard among us, than those of a good citizen, an open and resolute friend, and a virtuous supporter of the rights of mankind and of the free and independent states of America.

# THE SIEGE AND CAPTURE OF BOSTON

*Washington's Own Reports to the President of Congress*

*THE evacuation of Boston by the British forces under General Howe was the first military victory Washington achieved after taking command of the Continental Army. The town was besieged for nine months, and while great credit is given Washington for his strategy in fortifying Dorchester Heights, which commanded the town, Howe wrote a friend on March 21, 1776—four days after the evacuation—that he had received no instructions from his Government since the previous October and found his position intolerable.*

*One of his officers testifies that "we were seemingly abandoned by those who had sent us on so nefarious an expedition." Also that "the reason the rebels offered no obstruction to our retreat was for fear of our burning the town, which, had they fired a single shot, would have been done."*

*The President of Congress, to whom Washington writes during March, 1776, that "your house [in Boston] has received no damage worth mentioning," was John Hancock.*

ON THE 26th ultimo I had the honor of addressing you, and then mentioned that we were making preparations for taking possession of Dorchester Heights. I now beg leave to inform you, that a council of general officers having determined a previous bombardment and cannonade expedient and proper, in order to harass the enemy and divert their attention from that quarter, on Saturday, Sunday, and Monday nights last, we carried them on from our posts at Cobble Hill, Lechmere's Point, and Lamb's Dam. Whether they did the enemy any considerable and what injury, I have not yet heard, but have the pleasure to acquaint you, that they greatly facilitated our schemes, and would have been attended with success equal to our most sanguine expectations, had it not been for the unlucky bursting of two thirteen and three ten inch mortars, among which was the brass one taken in the ordnance brig. To what cause to attribute this misfortune, I know not; whether to any defects in them, or to the inexperience of the bombardiers.

But to return; on Monday evening, as soon as our firing commenced, a considerable detachment of our men, under the command of Brigadier-General Thomas, crossed the neck, and took possession of the two hills, without the least interruption or annoyance from the enemy; and by their great activity and industry, before the morning, advanced the works so far as to be secure against their shot. They are now going on with such expedition, that in a little time I hope they will be complete, and enable our troops stationed there to make a vigorous and obstinate stand. During the whole cannonade, which was incessant the two last nights, we were fortunate enough to lose but two men; one, a lieutenant, by a cannon-ball taking off his thigh; the other, a private, by the explosion of a shell, which also slightly wounded four or five more.

Our taking possession of Dorchester Heights is only preparatory to taking post on Nook's Hill, and the points opposite to the south end of Boston. It was absolutely necessary, that they should be previously fortified, in order to cover and command them.

As soon as the works on the former are finished, measures will be immediately adopted for securing the latter, and making them as strong and defensible as we can. Their contiguity to the enemy will make them of much importance and of great service to us. . . .

In case the ministerial troops have made an attempt to dislodge our men from Dorchester Hills, and the number detached upon the occasion had been so great as to have afforded a probability of a successful attack's being made upon Boston; on a signal given from Roxbury for that purpose, agreeably to a settled and concerted plan, four thousand chosen men, who were held in readiness, were to have embarked at the mouth of Cambridge River, in two divisions, the first under the command of Brigadier-General Sullivan, the second under Brigadier-General Greene; the whole to have been commanded by Major-General Putnam. The first division was to land at the powder-house and gain possession of Beacon Hill and Mount Horam; the second at Barton's Point, or a little south of it, and, after securing that post, to join the other division, and force the enemy's gates and works at the neck, for letting in the Roxbury troops. Three floating batteries were to have preceded, and gone in front of the other boats, and kept up a heavy fire on that part of the town where our men were to land. . . .

YESTERDAY evening a Captain Irvine who escaped from Boston the night before with six of his crew, came to headquarters and gave the following intelligence:

That our bombardment and cannonade caused a good deal of surprise and alarm in town, as many of the soldiery said they never heard or thought we had mortars or shell; that several of the officers acknowledged they were well and properly directed; that they made much distress and confusion; that the cannon shot for the greatest part went through the houses, and he was told that one took off the legs and arms of six men lying in the barracks on the Neck; that a soldier who came from the lines there on Tuesday morning informed him that 20 men had been wounded the night before. It was reported that others were also hurt, and one of the light horse torn to pieces by the explosion of a shell. This was afterwards contradicted. That early on Tuesday morning Admiral Shuldham discovering the works our people were throwing up on Dorchester Heights, immediately sent an express to General Howe to inform him, and that it was necessary they should be attacked and dislodged from thence, or he would be under the necessity of withdrawing the ships from the harbor, which were under his command; that preparations were directly made for that purpose as it was said, and from twelve to two o'clock about 3000 men embarked on board the transport which fell down to the Castle with a design of landing on that part of Dor-

chester next to it, and attacking the works on
the Heights at five o'clock next morning; that
Lord Percy was appointed to command; that
it was generally believed the attempt would
have been made, had it not been for the violent storm which happened that night, as I
have mentioned before; that he heard several
of the privates and one or two sergeants say
as they were embarking, that it would be another Bunker Hill affair.  He further informs
that the army is preparing to leave Boston,
and that they will do it in a day or two; that
the transports necessary for their embarkation
were getting ready with the utmost expedition; that there had been great movements
and confusion among the troops night and
day preceding his coming out, in hurrying
down their cannon, artillery and other stores
to the wharves with the utmost precipitation,
and were putting 'em on board the ships in
such haste that no account or memorandum
was taken of them; that most of the cannon
were removed from their works and embarked
or embarking; that he heard a woman say,
which he took to be an officer's wife, that she
had seen men go under the ground at the lines
on the Neck without returning; that the ship
he commanded was taken up, places fitted and
fitting for officers to lodge, and several shot,
shells and cannon already on board; that the
Tories were to have the liberty of going where
they please, if they can get seamen to man
the vessels, of which there was a great
scarcity; that on that account many vessels
could not be carried away and would be burnt;

that many of the inhabitants apprehended the town would be destroyed, and that it was generally thought their destination is Halifax. . . .

IN my letter of the 7th and 9th instant, which I had the honor of addressing you, I mentioned the intelligence I had received respecting the embarkation of the troops from Boston; and fully expected, before this, that the town would have been entirely evacuated. Although I have been deceived, and was rather premature in the opinion I had then formed, I have little reason to doubt that the event will take place in a very short time, as other accounts, which have come to hand since, the sailing of a great number of transports from the harbor to Nantasket Road, and many circumstances corresponding therewith, seem to confirm and render it unquestionable. Whether the town will be destroyed is a matter of much uncertainty; but it would seem, from the destruction they are making of sundry pieces of furniture, of many of their wagons and carts, which they cannot take with them as it is said, that it will not; for, if they intended it, the whole might be involved in one general ruin. . . .

IT IS with the greatest pleasure I inform you that on Sunday last, the 17th instant, about nine o'clock in the forenoon, the ministerial army evacuated the town of Boston, and that the forces of the United Colonies are now in actual possession thereof.

I beg leave to congratulate you, Sir, and the honorable Congress, on this happy event, and particularly as it was effected without endangering the lives and property of the remaining unhappy inhabitants.

I have great reason to imagine their flight was precipitated by the appearance of a work, which I had ordered to be thrown up last Saturday night on an eminence at Dorchester, which lies nearest to Boston Neck, called Nook's Hill. The town, although it has suffered greatly, is not in so bad a state as I expected to find it; and I have a particular pleasure in being able to inform you, Sir, that your house has received no damage worth mentioning. Your furniture is in tolerable order, and the family pictures are all left entire and untouched. Captain Cazneau takes charge of the whole, until he shall receive further orders from you.

As soon as the ministerial troops had quitted the town, I ordered a thousand men (who had had the smallpox), under command of General Putnam, to take possession of the heights, which I shall endeavor to fortify in such a manner, as to prevent their return, should they attempt it. But, as they are still in the harbor, I thought it not prudent to march off with the main body of the army, until I should be fully satisfied they had quitted the coast. I have, therefore, only detached five regiments, besides the rifle battalion, to New York, and shall keep the remainder here till all suspicion of their return ceases.

The situation in which I found their works evidently discovered, that their retreat was made with the greatest precipitation. They have left their barracks and other works of wood at Bunker's Hill all standing, and have destroyed but a small part of their lines. They have also left a number of fine pieces of cannon, which they first spiked up, also a very large iron mortar; and, (as I am informed,) they have thrown another over the end of your wharf. I have employed proper persons to drill the cannon, and doubt not I shall save the most of them. I am not yet able to procure an exact list of all the stores they have left. As soon as it can be done, I shall take care to transmit it to you. From an estimate of what the quartermaster-general has already discovered, the amount will be twenty-five or thirty thousand pounds.

Part of the powder mentioned in yours of the 6th instant has already arrived. The remainder I have ordered to be stopped on the road, as we shall have no occasion for it here. The letter to General Thomas, I immediately sent to him. He desired leave, for three or four days, to settle some of his private affairs; after which, he will set out for his command in Canada. I am happy that my conduct in intercepting Lord Drummond's letter is approved of by Congress. I have the honor to be, &c.

# THE WRITING OF THE DECLARATION OF INDEPENDENCE

## By Thomas Jefferson

*IN THIS illuminating letter to James Madison, written from Monticello during the administration and at the instance of President James Monroe, Thomas Jefferson corrects "a very careless and faulty statement" by John Adams of the circumstances attending the drafting of the Declaration. In so far as Jefferson wrote the Declaration and kept copious notes to refresh his memory, this undoubtedly is the correct and final word upon the subject.*

*A sensational charge of want of originality, which has been brought against the famous document, may here be noticed. Jefferson declares that while drafting it he consulted "neither book nor pamphlet," but that he did not consider it his business to "invent new ideas altogether."*

*Richard Henry Lee, one of the signers of the Declaration, who was most vociferous in charging plagiarism, is revealed in Randall's authoritative "Life of Jefferson" as having been responsible himself for the introduction of nearly all the alleged plagiarizations.*

I RECEIVED the enclosed letters from the President, with a request, that after perusal I would forward them to you, for perusal by yourself also, and to be returned then to him. You have doubtless seen Timothy Pickering's Fourth of July observations on the Declaration of Independence. If his principles and prejudices, personal and political, gave us no reason to doubt whether he had truly quoted the information he alleges to have received from Mr. Adams, I should then say, that in some of the particulars, Mr. Adams' memory has led him into unquestionable error. At the age of eighty-eight, and forty-seven years after the transactions of Independence, this is not wonderful. Nor

166

should I, at the age of eighty, on the small advantage of that difference only, venture to oppose my memory to his, were it not supported by written notes, taken by himself at the moment and on the spot.

He says, "the committee of five, to wit, Dr. Franklin, Sherman, Livingston, and ourselves, met, discussed the subject, and then appointed him and myself to make the draught; that we, as a sub-committee, met, and after the urgencies of each on the other, I consented to undertake the task; that the draught being made, we, the sub-committee, met, and conned the paper over, and he does not remember that he made or suggested a single alteration." Now these details are quite incorrect. The committee of five met; no such thing as a sub-committee was proposed, but they unanimously pressed on myself alone to undertake the draught. I consented; I drew it; but before I reported it to the committee, I communicated it separately to Dr. Franklin and Mr. Adams, requesting their corrections, because they were the two members of whose judgments and amendments I wished most to have the benefit, before presenting it to the committee; and you have seen the original paper now in my hands, with the corrections of Dr. Franklin and Mr. Adams interlined in their own handwritings. Their alterations were two or three only, and merely verbal. I then wrote a fair copy, reported it to the committee, and from them, unaltered, to Congress.

This personal communication and consultation with Mr. Adams, he has misremembered into the actings of a sub-committee.   Pickering's observations, and Mr. Adams' in addition, "that it contained no new ideas, that it is a common-place compilation, its sentiments hackneyed in Congress for two years before, and its essence contained in Otis' pamphlet," may all be true.   Of that I am not to be the judge.   Richard Henry Lee charged it as copied from Locke's treatise on government.   Otis' pamphlet I never saw, and whether I had gathered my ideas from reading or reflection I do not know.   I know only that I turned to neither book nor pamphlet while writing it.   I did not consider it as any part of my charge to invent new ideas altogether, and to offer no sentiment which had ever been expressed before.   Had Mr. Adams been so restrained, Congress would have lost the benefit of his bold and impressive advocations of the rights of Revolution.   For no man's confident and fervid addresses, more than Mr. Adams', encouraged and supported us through the difficulties surrounding us, which, like the ceaseless action of gravity, weighed on us by night and by day.   Yet, on the same ground, we may ask what of these elevated thoughts was new; or can be affirmed never before to have entered the conceptions of man?   Whether, also, the sentiments of Independence, and the reasons for declaring it, which make so great a portion of the instrument, had been hackneyed in Congress for two years before the 4th of July, '76, or this dictum also of Mr. Adams be another slip of memory, let history say.

This, however, I will say for Mr. Adams, that he supported the Declaration with zeal and ability, fighting fearlessly for every word of it. As to myself, I thought it a duty to be, on that occasion, a passive auditor of the opinions of others, more impartial judges than I could be, of its merits or demerits. During the debate I was sitting by Doctor Franklin, and he observed that I was writhing a little under the acrimonious criticisms on some of its parts; and it was on that occasion, that by way of comfort, he told me the story of John Thompson, the hatter, and his new sign. Timothy thinks the instrument the better for having a fourth of it expunged. He would have thought it still better, had the other three-fourths gone out also, all but the single sentiment (the only one he approved), which recommends friendship to his dear England, whenever she is willing to be at peace with us. His insinuations are, that although "the high tone of the instrument was in unison with the warm feelings of the times, this sentiment of habitual friendship to England should never be forgotten, and that the duties it enjoins should especially be borne in mind on every celebration of this anniversary." In other words, that the Declaration, as being a libel on the government of England, composed in times of passion, should now be buried in utter oblivion, to spare the feelings of our English friends and Angloman fellow-citizens. But it is not to wound them that we wish to keep it in mind; but to cherish the principles of the instrument in the bosoms of our own citizens; and it is a heavenly com-

fort to see that these principles are yet so strongly
felt, as to render a circumstance so trifling as this little
lapse of memory of Mr. Adams', worthy of being
solemnly announced and supported at an anniversary
assemblage of the nation on its birthday.   In opposition, however, to Mr. Pickering, I pray God that these
principles may be eternal, and close the prayer with
my affectionate wishes for yourself of long life, health
and happiness.

# JEFFERSON'S ORIGINAL DRAFT OF THE DECLARATION

*A Declaration by the Representatives of the United States of America, in General Congress Assembled*

*T*HE original copy of the Declaration of Independence, signed at Philadelphia, is preserved at the Patent Office in Washington. It is not divided into paragraphs, but dashes are inserted. The arrangement of paragraphs here followed is that adopted by John Dunlap, who printed the Declaration for the Continental Congress.

The same paragraphs are also made by Jefferson, in the original draft, preserved in the State Department. The names of the Colonies do not appear with those of the signers in the original.

The parts of the Declaration, as originally written, that were struck out by Congress are enclosed in brackets, and the amendments are indicated at the bottom of the page. It will be noticed that Congress almost completely rewrote the two concluding paragraphs, which are printed in parallel columns.

*W*HEN, in the course of human events, it becomes necessary for one people to dissolve the political bands which have connected them with another, and to assume among the powers of the earth the separate and equal station to which the laws of nature and of nature's God entitle them, a decent respect to the opinions of mankind requires that they should declare the causes which impel them to the separation.

We hold these truths to be self-evident: that all men are created equal; that they are endowed by their creator with [inherent and] [1] inalienable rights; that among these are life, liberty, and the pursuit of happiness; that to secure these rights, governments

[1] certain

171

are instituted among men, deriving their just powers
from the consent of the governed; that whenever any
form of government becomes destructive of these
ends, it is the right of the people to alter or to abolish
it, and to institute new government laying its foundation on such principles, and organizing its powers in
such form, as to them shall seem most likely to effect
their safety and happiness.  Prudence, indeed, will
dictate that governments long established should not
be changed for light and transient causes; and accordingly all experience hath shown that mankind are
more disposed to suffer while evils are sufferable, than
to right themselves by abolishing the forms to which
they are accustomed.  But when a long train of abuses
and usurpations [begun at a distinguished period and]
pursuing invariably the same object, evinces a design
to reduce them under absolute despotism, it is their
right, it is their duty to throw off such government,
and to provide new guards for their future security.
Such has been the patient sufferance of these Colonies; and such is now the necessity which constrains
them to [expunge] [1] their former systems of government.  The history of the present King of Great Britain is a history of [unremitting] [2] injuries and usurpations, [among which appears no solitary fact to contradict the uniform tenor of the rest, but all have] [3]
in direct object the establishment of an absolute
tyranny over these States.  To prove this, let facts be

[1] alter          [2] repeated          [3] all having

submitted to a candid world [for the truth of which we pledge a faith yet unsullied by falsehood].

He has refused his assent to laws the most wholesome and necessary for the public good.

He has forbidden his governors to pass laws of immediate and pressing importance, unless suspended in their operation till his assent should be obtained; and, when so suspended, he has utterly neglected to attend to them.

He has refused to pass other laws for the accommodation of large districts of people, unless those people would relinquish the right of representation in the Legislature, a right inestimable to them, and formidable to tyrants only.

He has called together legislative bodies at places unusual, uncomfortable, and distant from the depository of their public records, for the sole purpose of fatiguing them into compliance with his measures.

He has dissolved representative houses repeatedly [and continually] for opposing with manly firmness his invasions on the rights of the people.

He has refused for a long time after such dissolutions to cause others to be elected, whereby the legislative powers, incapable of annihilation, have returned to the people at large for their exercise, the State remaining, in the meantime, exposed to all the dangers of invasion from without and convulsions within.

He has endeavored to prevent the population of these States; for that purpose obstructing the laws for naturalization of foreigners, refusing to pass others to encourage their migrations hither, and raising the conditions of new appropriations of lands.

He has [suffered] [1] the administration of justice [totally to cease in some of these States] [2] refusing his assent to laws for establishing judiciary powers.

He has made [our] judges dependent on his will alone for the tenure of their offices, and the amount and payment of their salaries.

He has erected a multitude of new offices, [by a self-assumed power] and sent hither swarms of new officers to harass our people and eat out their substance.

He has kept among us in times of peace standing armies [and ships of war] without the consent of our Legislatures.

He has affected to render the military independent of, and superior to, the civil power.

He has combined with others to subject us to a jurisdiction foreign to our constitutions and unacknowledged by our laws, giving his assent to their acts of pretended legislation for quartering large bodies of armed troops among us; for protecting them by a mock trial from punishment for any murders which they should commit on the inhabitants of these States; for cutting off our trade with all parts of the world; for imposing taxes on us without our consent; for depriving us [] [3] of the benefits of trial by jury; for transporting us beyond seas to be tried for pre-

---

[1] obstructed          [2] by          [3] in many cases

tended offences; for abolishing the free system of English laws in a neighboring province, establishing therein an arbitrary government, and enlarging its boundaries, so as to render it at once an example and fit instrument for introducing the same absolute rule into these [States] [1]; for taking away our charters, abolishing our most valuable laws, and altering fundamentally the forms of our governments; for suspending our own Legislatures, and declaring themselves invested with power to legislate for us in all cases whatsoever.

He has abdicated government here [withdrawing his governors, and declaring us out of his allegiance and protection].[2]

He has plundered our seas, ravaged our coasts, burnt our towns, and destroyed the lives of our people.

He is at this time transporting large armies of foreign mercenaries to complete the works of death, desolation, and tyranny already begun with circumstances of cruelty and perfidy [] [3] unworthy the head of a civilized nation.

He has constrained our fellow-citizens taken captive on the high seas to bear arms against their country, to become the executioners of their friends and brethren, or to fall themselves by their hands.

He has [] [4] endeavored to bring on the inhabitants of our frontiers the merciless Indian savages, whose

[1] Colonies
[2] by declaring us out of his protection, and waging war against us.
[3] scarcely paralleled in the most barbarous ages, and totally
[4] excited domestic insurrection among us, and has

known rule of warfare is an undistinguished destruction of all ages, sexes, and conditions [of existence].

[He has incited treasonable insurrections of our fellow-citizens, with the allurements for forfeiture and confiscation of our property.

He has waged cruel war against human nature itself, violating its most sacred rights of life and liberty in the persons of a distant people who never offended him, captivating and carrying them into slavery in another hemisphere, or to incur miserable death in their transportation thither. This piratical warfare, the opprobrium of infidel powers, is the warfare of the Christian King of Great Britain. Determined to keep open a market where men should be bought and sold, he has prostituted his negative for suppressing every legislative attempt to prohibit or to restrain this execrable commerce. And that this assemblage of horrors might want no fact of distinguished die, he is now exciting those very people to rise in arms among us, and to purchase that liberty of which he has deprived them, by murdering the people on whom he also obtruded them: thus paying off former crimes committed against the liberties of one people with crimes which he urges them to commit against the lives of another.]

In every stage of these oppressions we have petitioned for redress in the most humble terms: our repeated petitions have been answered only by repeated injuries.

SIGNING THE DECLARATION OF INDEPENDENCE (*From Trumbull's painting in the rotunda of the Capitol at Washington*)

A Prince whose character is thus marked by every act which may define a tyrant is unfit to be the ruler of a [] [1] people [who mean to be free. Future ages will scarcely believe that the hardiness of one man adventured, within the short compass of twelve years only, to lay a foundation so broad and so undisguised for tyranny over a people fostered and fixed in principles of freedom.]

Nor have we been wanting in attentions to our British brethren. We have warned them from time to time of attempts by their legislature to extend [a] [2] jurisdiction over [these our States].[3] We have reminded them of the circumstances of our emigration and settlement here, [no one of which could warrant so strange a pretension: that these were effected at the expense of our own blood and treasure, unassisted by the wealth or the strength of Great Britain: that in constituting indeed our several forms of government, we had adopted one common king, thereby laying a foundation for perpetual league and amity with them: but that submission to their parliament was no part of our Constitution, nor ever in idea, if history may be credited: and,] we [] [4] appealed to their native justice and magnanimity [as well as to] [5] the ties of our common kindred to disavow these usurpations which [were likely to] [6] interrupt our connection and correspondence. They

[1] free     [2] an unwarrantable     [3] us     [4] have
[5] and we have conjured them by
[6] would inevitably

too have been deaf to the voice of justice and of consanguinity, [ and when occasions have been given them, by the regular course of their laws, of removing from their councils the disturbers of our harmony, they have, by their free election, reëstablished them in power. At this very time too, they are permitting their chief magistrate to send over not only soldiers of our common blood, but Scotch and foreign mercenaries to invade and destroy us. These facts have given the last stab to agonizing affection, and manly spirit bids us to renounce forever these unfeeling brethren. We must endeavor to forget our former love for them, and hold them as we hold the rest of mankind, enemies in war, in peace friends. We might have been a free and a great people together; but a communication of grandeur and of freedom, it seems, is below their dignity. Be it so, since they will have it. The road to happiness and to glory is open to us too. We will tread it apart from them, and] [1] acquiesce in the necessity which denounces our [eternal] separation [] [2]!

| | |
|---|---|
| We therefore the representatives of the United States of America in General Congress assembled, appealing to the supreme judge of the world for the rectitude of our intentions, do in the name, and | We therefore the representatives of the United States of America in General Congress assembled, do in the name, and by the authority of the good people of these [States reject and renounce all |

[1] We must therefore

[2] and hold them as we hold the rest of mankind, enemies of war, in peace friends.

by the authority of the good people of these Colonies, solemnly publish and declare, that these united Colonies are, and of right ought to be, free and independent States; that they are absolved from all allegiance to the British crown, and that all political connection between them and the state of Great Britain is, and ought to be, totally dissolved; and that as free and independent States, they have full power to levy war, conclude peace, contract alliances, establish commerce, and to do all other acts and things which independent States may of right do.

And for the support of this declaration, with a firm reliance on the protection of divine providence, we mutually pledge to each other our lives, our fortunes, and our sacred honor.

allegiance and subjection to the kings of Great Britain and all others who may hereafter claim by, through, or under them; we utterly dissolve all political connection which may heretofore have subsisted between us and the people or parliament of Great Britain: and finally we do assert and declare these Colonies to be free and independent States,] and that as free and independent States, they have full power to levy war, conclude peace, contract alliances, establish commerce, and to do all other acts and things which independent States may of right do.

And for the support of this declaration, we mutually pledge to each other our lives, our fortunes, and our sacred honor.

# WHY JEFFERSON WAS CHOSEN TO WRITE THE DECLARATION

## By John Adams

*IN WRITING this letter to Timothy Pickering forty-six years after the Declaration of Independence was drafted, John Adams did a service not only to its recipient, who had been his Secretary of State, but to posterity. Why, indeed, did the Continental Congress of many graybeards choose Jefferson, a young man of thirty-three, to draft so grave and revolutionary a document? One reason, which Adams neglects to state, was that Jefferson had some time previously written in pamphlet form "A Summary View of the Rights of British America," which provoked the British Government to name its author in a bill to punish sedition. In drafting the famous Declaration, Jefferson simply revised and elaborated the earlier document to suit the greater occasion.*

*Pickering was successively Postmaster-General of the United States, Secretary of War, as well as of State, and United States Senator.*

YOU inquire why so young a man as Mr. Jefferson was placed at the head of the Committee for preparing a Declaration of Independence? I answer: It was the Frankfort advice, to place Virginia at the head of everything. Mr. Richard Henry Lee might be gone to Virginia, to his sick family, for aught I know, but that was not the reason of Mr. Jefferson's appointment. There were three committees appointed at the same time. One for the Declaration of Independence, another for preparing articles of Confederation, and another for preparing a treaty to be proposed to France. Mr. Lee was chosen for the Committee of Confederation, and it was not thought convenient that the same person should be upon both.

Mr. Jefferson came into Congress, in June, 1775, and brought with him a reputation for literature, science, and a happy talent for composition. Writings of his were handed about, remarkable for the peculiar felicity of expression. Though a silent member in Congress, he was so prompt, frank, explicit, and decisive upon committees and in conversation, not even Samuel Adams was more so, that he soon seized upon my heart; and upon this occasion I gave him my vote, and did all in my power to procure the votes of others. I think he had one more vote than any other, and that placed him at the head of the committee. I had the next highest number, and that placed me the second. The committee met, discussed the subject, and then appointed Mr. Jefferson and me to make the draft, I suppose because we were the two first on the list.

The sub-committee met. Jefferson proposed to me to make the draft. I said, "I will not." "You should do it." "Oh! no." "Why will you not? You ought to do it." "I will not." "Why?" "Reasons enough." "What can be your reasons?" "Reason first—You are a Virginian, and a Virginian ought to appear at the head of this business. Reason second—I am obnoxious, suspected and unpopular. You are very much otherwise. Reason third—You can write ten times better than I can." "Well," said Jefferson, "if you are decided, I will do as well as I can." "Very well. When you have drawn it up, we will have a meeting."

A meeting we accordingly had, and conned the paper over. I was delighted with its high tone and the flights of oratory with which it abounded, especially that concerning negro slavery, which, though I knew his Southern brethren would never suffer to pass in Congress, I certainly never would oppose. There were other expressions which I would not have inserted, if I had drawn it up, particularly that which called the King tyrant. I thought this too personal; for I never believed George to be a tyrant in disposition and in nature; I always believed him to be deceived by his courtiers on both sides of the Atlantic, and in his official capacity only, cruel. I thought the expression too passionate, and too much like scolding, for so grave and solemn a document; but as Franklin and Sherman were to inspect it afterwards, I thought it would not become me to strike it out. I consented to report it, and do not now remember that I made or suggested a single alteration.

We reported it to the committee of five. It was read, and I do not remember that Franklin or Sherman criticised anything. We were all in haste. Congress was impatient, and the instrument was reported, as I believed, in Jefferson's handwriting, as he first drew it. Congress cut off about a quarter of it, as I expected they would; but they obliterated some of the best of it, and left all that was exceptionable, if anything in it was. I have long wondered that the original draft has not been published. I suppose the reason is, the vehement philippic against negro slavery.

As you justly observe, there is not an idea in it but what had been hackneyed in Congress for two years before. The substance of it is contained in the declaration of rights and the violation of those rights, in the Journals of Congress, in 1774. Indeed, the essence of it is contained in a pamphlet, voted and printed by the town of Boston, before the first Congress met, composed by James Otis, as I suppose, in one of his lucid intervals, and pruned and polished by Samuel Adams.

6 *August,* 1822,

# THE MECKLENBURG DECLARATION OF INDEPENDENCE

*THIS much-disputed set of resolutions purporting to have been adopted in Mecklenburg County, North Carolina, May 20, 1775—the day after the receipt of the news of the Battle of Lexington—by a convention of delegates representing each militia company of the county, was believed by Thomas Jefferson to be a fabrication. It was first published in the Raleigh (N. C.) Register on April 30, 1819, from what was said to be a copy made from recollection of the original which had been destroyed by fire forty-four years previously.*

*Similarity of phrases in the two documents is striking. "How is it possible," wrote John Adams to Jefferson (June 22, 1819), "that this paper should have been concealed from me to this day Had I possessed it I would have made the Halls of Congress reëcho with it fifteen months before your Declaration of Independence." In 1819 many old citizens of Mecklenburg County remembered to have heard of such a declaration.*

1. RESOLVED, That whosoever directly or indirectly abetted or in any way, form, or manner, countenanced the unchartered and dangerous invasion of our rights, as claimed by Great Britain, is an enemy to this Country—to America—and to the inherent and inalienable rights of man.

2. **Resolved,** That we the citizens of Mecklenburg County, do hereby dissolve the political bands which have connected us to the Mother Country, and hereby absolve ourselves from all allegiance to the British Crown and abjure all political connection, contract, or association, with that Nation, who have wantonly trampled on our rights and liberties—and inhumanly shed the innocent blood of American patriots at Lexington.

3.  **Resolved,** That we do hereby declare ourselves a free and independent people, are, and of a right ought to be, a sovereign and self-governing Association, under the control of no power, other than that of our God and the General Government of the Congress; to the maintenance of which independence, we solemnly pledge to each other, our mutual coöperation, our lives, our fortunes, and our most sacred honor.

4.  **Resolved,** That as we now acknowledge the existence and control of no law or legal officer, civil or military, within this County, we do hereby ordain and adopt, as a rule of life, all, each and every of our former laws—wherein, nevertheless, the Crown of Great Britain never can be considered as holding rights, privileges, immunities, or authority therein.

5.  **Resolved,** That it is also further decreed, that all, each and every military officer in this County, is hereby reinstated to his former command and authority, he acting conformably to these regulations, and that every member present of this delegation shall henceforth be a civil officer, viz. a Justice of the Peace, in the character of a "Committee-man," to issue process, hear and determine all matters of controversy, according to said adopted laws, and to preserve peace, and union, and harmony, in said County, and to use every exertion to spread the love of country and fire of freedom throughout America, until a more general and organized government be established in this province.

# THE BATTLE OF LONG ISLAND

## By a British Field-Officer

'*THIS letter from a royal field-officer, serving under General Howe at the Battle of Long Island, to his wife at Gloucester, England, is dated from the English camp on Long Island, September 1, 1776, and describes the first serious defeat the American forces suffered during the Revolutionary War. It is one in a collection of newly discovered "Letters on the American Revolution" (Houghton - Mifflin) edited by Margaret Wheeler Willard.*

*Strongly entrenched on Brooklyn Heights, the Americans numbered some 8,000 men under General Israel Putnam. The British force under General Howe was nearly twice as strong, and succeeded in storming the American position, inflicting an American loss of about 1,000 in killed, wounded and missing, as contrasted to 400 fatalities of their own. General Washington hurried to Long Island from the mainland after the battle, and on the night of August 29-30 he successfully transported the colonial troops.*

WE HAVE had a glorious day against the rebels. We landed on this island the 22d, and that day marched toward Brookland Ferry, opposite New York, where this island is separated from the town by the East River, which is about three quarters of a mile over.

We took post within musket shot of their unfinished works. The troops were all on fire to force their lines, but Gen. Howe, in whose conduct the utmost prudence and vigilance have been united, would not permit it.

It was not till eight o'clock at night on the 26th that we received our orders to attack, and at eleven the whole army was in motion. The reserve, commanded by Lord Cornwallis, the first brigade of which our regiment makes a part, and the light infantry of the army, the whole under the command of General Clinton, marched by the right. The road to the right, after a march of about seven miles, brought us to an easy and undefended ascent of the hills, which we possessed at daybreak, and continued our rout, gained the rear of the rebels: and while the Hessians and the rest of the army amused them in front and on the left, the grenadiers and light infantry attacked them in the rear: by this masterly maneuver the rebels were immediately thrown into general confusion, and behaved most shamefully. The numbers killed, wounded, and taken you will see in the Gazette. Some of the Hessians told me they had buried between 400 and 500 in one pit.

Such has been their panic that, on the 30th at night, they evacuated their redoubts and entrenchments, which they had retired to, on Brookland Heights, leaving us in possession of this island, which entirely commands New York. Had the works at Brookland been properly defended our motions must have been retarded at least three weeks. For my part I think matters will soon be brought to an issue.

P.S. I have just heard there has been a most dreadful fray in the town of New York. The New Englanders insisted upon setting the town on fire, and retreating. This was opposed by the New Yorkers, who were joined by the Pennsylvanians, and a battle has been the consequence in which many have lost their lives.

By the steps the General is taking, I imagine he will effectually cut off their retreat at King's Bridge, by which the island of New York is joined to the continent.

# THE EVACUATION OF NEW YORK

## By General George Clinton

*GENERAL, later to be for eighteen years Governor, Clinton, here describes a brisk skirmish between the American and British forces on Manhattan Island in 1776, a short time before the town was abandoned to the enemy. It was a dark hour for the struggling colonies, and it is significant that such a slight success as this one reanimated the American troops, recently disheartened by their defeat on Long Island, preceding the defeat at White Plains and the massacre at Fort Washington.*

*A year later General Clinton was elected first Governor of New York, and from 1805 until his death in 1812 he was Vice-President of the United States. He opposed the ratification of the Federal Constitution as granting too great powers to national officials, and while presiding officer of the Senate he defeated by his deciding vote the re-chartering of the United States Bank.*

ABOUT the middle of last week it was determined, for many reasons, to evacuate the City of New York; and accordingly, orders were given for removing the ordnance, military and other stores from thence, which, by Sunday morning was nearly effected. On Saturday, four of the enemy's large ships passed by the city up the North River, and anchored near Grenage, and about as many up the East River, which anchored in Turtle Bay; and from the movements of the enemy on Long Island, and the small Islands in the East River, we had great reason to apprehend they intended to make a landing, and attack our lines somewhere near the city. Our army for some days had been moving upwards this way, and encamping on the heights, southwest of Colonel Morris's, where

we intended to form lines, and make our grand stand.
On Sunday morning the enemy landed a very considerable body of troops, principally consisting of
their Light Infantry and Grenadiers, near Turtle Bay,
under cover of a very heavy cannonade from their
shipping. Our lines were but thinly manned, as they
were then intended only to secure a retreat to the
rear of our army, and unfortunately by such troops
as were so little disposed to stand in the way of grape-
shot that the main body of them almost instantly retreated, nay, fled, without a possibility of rallying
them, though General Washington himself, (who
rode to the spot on hearing the cannonade) with some
other general officers, exerted themselves to effect it.

The enemy, on landing, immediately formed a line
across the island. Most of our people were luckily
north of it, and joined the army. The few that were
in the city crossed the river, chiefly to Paulus-Hook,
so that our loss in men, artillery, or stores, is very inconsiderable; I don't believe it exceeds one hundred
men, and I fancy most of them, from their conduct,
stayed out of choice. Before evening, the enemy
landed the main body of their army, took possession
of the city, and marched up the island, and encamped
on the heights extending from McGowan's and the
Black-Horse to the North River.

On Monday morning, about ten o'clock, a party
of the enemy, consisting of Highlanders, Hessians,
the Light Infantry, Grenadiers, and English troops,
(number uncertain,) attacked our advanced party,

commanded by Colonel Knowlton, at Martje Davit's
Fly.  They were opposed with spirit, and soon made
to retreat to a clear field, southwest of that about two
hundred paces, where they lodged themselves behind
a fence covered with bushes.  Our people attacked
them in front, and caused them to retreat a second
time, leaving five dead on the spot.  We pursued them
to a buckwheat field on the top of a high hill, distant
about four hundred paces, where they received a considerable reinforcement, with several field-pieces, and
there made a stand.  A very brisk action ensued at
this place, which continued about two hours.  Our
people at length worsted them a third time, caused
them to fall back into an orchard, from thence across
a hollow, and up another hill not far distant from
their own lines.  A large column of the enemy's army
being at this time discovered to be in motion, and
the ground we then occupied being rather disadvantageous, a retreat likewise, without bringing on a general action, (which we did not think prudent to risk,)
rather insecure, our party was therefore ordered in,
and the enemy was well contented to hold the last
ground we drove them to.

We lost, on this occasion, Colonel Knowlton, a
brave officer, and sixteen privates, killed.  Major
Leitch, from Virginia, and about eight or ten subaltern officers and privates wounded.  The loss of
the enemy is uncertain.  They carried their dead and
wounded off, in and soon after the action; but we
have good evidence of their having upwards of sixty

killed, and violent presumption of one hundred. The action, in the whole, lasted about four hours.

I consider our success in this small affair, at this time, almost equal to a victory. It has animated our troops, gave them new spirits, and erased every bad impression the retreat from Long Island, &c., had left on their minds. They find they are able, with inferior numbers, to drive their enemy, and think of nothing now but conquest.

Since the above affair, nothing material has happened. The enemy keep close to their lines. Our advance parties continue at their former station. We are daily throwing up works to prevent the enemy's advancing. Great attention is paid to Fort Washington, the posts opposite to it on the Jersey shore, and the obstructions in the river, which, I have reason to believe, are already effectual, so as to prevent their shipping passing; however, it is intended still to add to them, as it is of the utmost consequence to keep the enemy below us.

# THE BATTLE OF WHITE PLAINS

## By General William Heath

*THE first of these two letters, which give the best extant eye-witness description of the Battle of White Plains, was written by General Heath, one of the American commanders in that engagement, October 27, 1776; and the second letter, dated from White Plains, N. Y., November 1, 1776, and evidently written by a soldier in the American ranks, was printed in the Pennsylvania Evening Post of November 14, 1776.*

*Heath, who refers to himself in the third person, had been made a major-general shortly before the White Plains engagement, and subsequently was in command of the Hudson River posts. The position which the Americans first occupied at White Plains was Chatterton Hill, from which General McDougall was forced to withdraw. Lord Howe delayed his attack on the main American army, and on the evening of November 31 Washington took up an unassailable position at North Castle. Clouds were rapidly darkening the American outlook at this time.*

IN THE forenoon [October 27, 1776] a heavy cannonade was heard towards Fort Washington. Thirteen Hessians and two or three British soldiers were sent in on this day.

From the American camp to the southwest there appeared to be a very commanding height, worthy of attention. The Commander-in-Chief ordered the general officers who were off duty to attend him, to reconnoitre this ground, on this morning. When arrived at the ground, although very commanding, it did not appear so much so as other grounds to the north, and almost parallel with the left of the army as it was then formed. "Yonder," says Major-General Lee, pointing to the grounds just mentioned, "is the ground we ought to

193

occupy." "Let us, then, go and view it," replied the Commander-in-Chief. When on the way, a Light-Horseman came up in full gallop, his horse almost out of breath, and addressed General Washington, "The British are on the camp, sir." The General observed, "Gentlemen, we have now other business than reconnoitring," putting his horse in full gallop for the camp, and followed by the other officers. When arrived at headquarters, the Adjutant-General, (Reed,) who had remained at camp, informed the Commander-in-Chief that the guards had been all beat in, and the whole American army were now at their respective posts, in order of battle. The Commander-in-Chief turned round to the officers, and only said, "Gentlemen, you will repair to your respective posts, and do the best you can." General Heath, on arriving at his own division, found them all in the lines; and, from the height of his post, found that the first attack was directed against the Americans on Chaderton's hill. The little river Brunx, which ran between the American right and this hill, after running round its north side, turned and ran down on the east and southeast. The British advanced in two columns.

At this instant, the cannonade was brisk on both sides, directed by the British across the hollow and Brunx, against the Americans on the hill, and by them returned. Almost at the same instant, the right column, composed of British troops, preceded by about twenty Light-Horse, in full gallop, and brandishing their swords, appeared on the road leading to the Court-House, and now directly in front of General Heath's division. The Light-Horse leaped the fence of a wheat-field at the foot of the hill, on which Colonel Malcom's regiment was posted, of which the Light-Horse were not aware, until a shot from Lieutenant Fenno's field-piece gave them notice, by striking in the midst of them, and a horseman pitching from his horse. They then wheeled short about, galloped out of the field as fast they came in, rode behind a little hill in the road, and faced about, the tops of their caps only being visible to General Heath where he stood. The column came no further up the road, but wheeled to the left by platoons, as they came up, and, passing through a bar or gateway, directed their head towards the troops on Chaderton's hill, now engaged. When the head of the column had got nearly across the lot, their front got out of sight; nor could the extent of their rear be now discovered.

The sun shone bright, their arms glittered, and perhaps troops never were shown to more advantage than these now appeared. The whole now halted, and, for a few minutes, the men all sat down in the same order in which they stood, no one appearing to move out of his place. The cannonade continued brisk across the Brunx. A part of the left column, composed of British and Hessians, forded the river, and marched along, under the cover of the hill, until they had gained sufficient ground to the left of the

Americans, when, by facing to the left, their column became a line parallel with the Americans. When they briskly ascended the hill, the first column resumed a quick march. As the troops which were advancing to the attack ascended the hill, the cannonade on the side of the British ceased, as their own men became exposed to their fire if continued. The fire of small-arms was now very heavy, and without any distinction of sounds. This led some American officers who were looking on to observe that the British were worsted, as their cannon had ceased firing; but a few minutes evinced that the Americans were giving way. They moved off the hill in a great body, neither running nor observing the best order. The British ascended the hill very slowly, and when arrived at its summit, formed and dressed their line, without the least attempt to pursue the Americans. The loss on the side of the Americans was inconsiderable; that of the British was not then known. The British having got possession of this hill, it gave them a vast advantage of the American lines, almost down to the center. . . .

LAST Monday we received intelligence that the enemy, with their whole body, were advancing towards us. The army were immediately alarmed, and part of General Wadsworth's brigade, with some other regiments under the command of General Spencer, consisting in the whole of five or six hundred men, were sent out as an advance party, to skirmish with the enemy, and harass them in their march. We marched on to a hill about one mile and a half from our lines, with an artillery company and two field-pieces, and placed ourselves behind walls and fences, in the best manner we could, to give the enemy trouble. About half after nine o'clock, our advance parties all came in, retreating before the enemy; and the light parties of the enemy, with their advanced guard, consisting of two or three thousand, came in sight, and marched on briskly towards us, keeping the high grounds; and the light horse pranced on a little in the rear, making a very martial appearance.

As our light parties came on to the hills and discovered where we were, the enemy began to cannonade us, and to fling shells from their hobits and small mortars. Their light parties soon came on, and we firing upon them from the walls and fences, broke and scattered them at once; but they would run from our front and get round upon our wings to flank us, and as soon as our fire discovered where we were, the enemy's artillery would at once begin to play upon us in the most furious manner. We kept the walls until the enemy were just ready to surround us, and then we would retreat from one wall and hill to another, and maintain our ground there in the same manner, till numbers were just ready to surround us. Once the Hessian grenadiers came up in front of Colonel Douglass's regiment, and we fired a general volley upon them, at about twenty rods distance, and scattered them like leaves in a whirlwind;

and they ran off so far that some of the regiment ran out to the ground where they were when we fired upon them, and brought off their arms and accoutrements, and rum, that the men who fell had with them, which we had time to drink round with before they came on again.  They formed at a distance, and waited until their artillery and main body came on, when they advanced in solid columns upon us, and were gathering all around us, ten to our one.  Colonel Douglass's and Silliman's regiments fired four or five times on them, as they were advancing and then retreated, but not until the enemy began to fire on their flanks.  Colonels Silliman, Douglass, and Arnold behaved nobly, and the men gained much applause.  Colonels Webb's, Silliman's, and Douglass's regiments had the principal share in the action.  Colonel Webb had four killed, and eight or ten wounded; Colonel Silliman lost six, and had ten or twelve wounded; Colonel Douglass had three killed, and six wounded.  Colonels Brooks's, Smallwood's, and Ritzma's regiments, who were drawn up on the hill near the lines, suffered considerably.  Our loss in the whole may be seventy or eighty killed or wounded. It is said by all the deserters and captains, who agree in their stories, that the enemy had about three hundred killed and wounded.

The scene was grand and solemn; all the adjacent hills smoked as though on fire, and bellowed and trembled with a perpetual cannonade and fire of field-pieces, hobits, and mortars.  The air groaned with streams of cannon and musket shot; the hills smoked and echoed terribly with the bursting of shells; the fences and walls were knocked down and torn to pieces, and men's legs, arms, and bodies, mangled with cannon and grape-shot all around us. I was in the action, and under as good advantages as any one man, perhaps, to observe all that passed, and write these particulars of the action from my own observation.

No general action was designed on our part, and I believe one thousand men were never, at one time, engaged with the enemy. They came on to the hills opposite our lines, and halted; and after cannonading part of the lines a short time, they became very still and quiet.

Yesterday, (October 31st,) it was observed that they had near finished four or five batteries which they had erected against us; and as our ground, near the center of the town at White Plains, was not good, being overlooked by neighboring hills, the generals, last night, drew off most of the troops from the lines there, and this morning the guards and sentries burned the town and forage all around it, and came off about nine o'clock.

We carried off all our stores, and planted our artillery on the hills about a mile and a half back of the center of the town. The enemy advanced, this forenoon, on to the ground we left, but as soon as they came over the hill, we saluted them with our cannon and field-pieces, and they advanced no further. . . .

# WASHINGTON, DISCOURAGED, APPEALS TO CONGRESS

*OF EXCEPTIONAL inter-est are these two letters, written to Washington's brother, Augustine, and to John Han-cock, President of Congress, De-cember 18 and 20, 1776, in that they reveal the desperate plight of the American cause in those dark days and the in-domitable spirit of the author. Following the defeats on Long Island and at White Plains, Washington had been hotly pur-sued through New Jersey by the British, and when he crossed the Delaware into Pennsylvania he had less than 3,000 weary, half-starved, dispirited soldiers.*

*The tide turned with his cap-ture of 1,000 Hessians at Tren-ton, and by March, 1777, Washington had not only saved his army but had inspired the despairing colonists with renewed hope and Congress with such con-fidence in him that almost dicta-torial powers were conferred upon Washington. Nothing but his iron resolution prevented the collapse of the Revolution.*

OWING to the num-ber of letters, I write, the recollection of any particular one is de-stroyed, but I think my last to you was by Colonel Woodford, from Hackin-sac. Since that time, and a little before, our affairs have taken an adverse turn, but not more than was to be expected from the unfortunate meas-ures, which had been adopted for the establish-ment of our army. The retreat of the enemy from White Plains led me to think, that they would turn their thoughts to the Jerseys, if no farther, and induced me to cross the North River with some of the troops in order if pos-sible to oppose them. I expected to have met at least five thousand men of the Flying Camp and militia; instead of which I found less than one half of that

number, and no disposition in the inhabitants to afford
the least aid. This being perfectly well known to the
enemy, they threw over a large body of troops, which
pushed us from place to place, till we were obliged to
cross the Delaware with less than three thousand men
fit for duty, owing to the dissolution of our force by
short enlistments; the enemy's numbers, from the
best accounts, exceeding ten or twelve thousand
men. . . .

. . . We are in a very disaffected part of the province; and, between you and me, I think our affairs
are in a very bad situation; not so much from the apprehension of General Howe's army, as from the
defection of New York, Jerseys and Pennsylvania. . . .

I have no doubt but General Howe will still make
an attempt upon Philadelphia this winter. I see nothing to oppose him a fortnight hence, as the time of
all the troops, except those of Virginia reduced (almost to nothing,) and Smallwood's Regiment of
Maryland, equally as bad, will expire in less than that
time. In a word, my dear Sir, if every nerve is not
strained to recruit the new army with all possible
expedition, I think the game is pretty near up, owing,
in a great measure, to the insidious arts of the enemy,
and disaffection of the colonies before mentioned, but
principally to the accursed policy of short enlistments,
and placing too great a dependence on the militia, the
evil consequences of which were foretold fifteen
months ago, with a spirit almost prophetic. Before
this reaches you, you will no doubt have heard of the

captivity of General Lee. This is an additional misfortune, and the more vexatious, as it was by his own
folly and imprudence, (and without a view to answer
any good,) he was taken, going three miles out of
his own camp, and within twenty of the enemy to
lodge, a rascally Tory rode in the night to give notice
of it to the enemy, who sent a party of Light-Horse
that seized and carried him, with every mark of
triumph and indignity.

You can form no idea of the perplexity of my situation. No man, I believe, ever had a greater choice
of difficulties, and less means to extricate himself
from them. However, under a full persuasion of the
justice of our cause, I cannot entertain an idea, that
it will finally sink, though it may remain for some
time under a cloud. . . .

## TO THE PRESIDENT OF CONGRESS

THE pay of our artillerists bearing no proportion
to that in the English and French service, the
murmuring and dissatisfaction thereby occasioned,
the absolute impossibility, as I am told, of getting
them upon the old terms, and the unavoidable necessity of obtaining them at all events, have induced me,
also by advice, to promise officers and men, that their
pay shall be augmented twenty-five per cent, or that
their engagements shall become null and void. This
may appear to Congress premature and unwarrantable. But, Sir, if they view our situation in the light

it strikes their officers, they will be convinced of the utility of the measure, and that the execution could not be delayed till after their meeting at Baltimore. In short, the present exigency of our affairs will not admit of delay, either in council or the field; for well convinced I am, that, if the enemy go into quarters at all, it will be for a short season. But I rather think the design of General Howe is to possess himself of Philadelphia this winter, if possible; and in truth I do not see what is to prevent him, as ten days more will put an end to the existence of our army. That one great point is to keep us as much harassed as possible, with a view to injure the recruiting service and hinder a collection of stores and other necessaries for the next campaign, I am as clear in, as I am of my existence. If, therefore, we have to provide in the short interval and make these great and arduous preparations, every matter that in its nature is self-evident is to be referred to Congress, at the distance of a hundred and thirty or forty miles, so much time must necessary elapse, as to defeat the end in view.

It may be said, that this is an application for powers that are too dangerous to be entrusted. I can only add, that desperate diseases require desperate remedies; and I with truth declare, that I have no lust after power, but I wish with as much fervency as any man upon this wide-extended continent for an opportunity of turning the sword into the ploughshare. But my feelings, as an officer and a man, have been such as to force me to say, that no person ever had a greater choice of difficulties to contend with than I have. It is needless to add, that short enlistments, and a mistaken dependence upon militia, have been the origin of all our misfortunes, and the great accumulation of our debt. We find, Sir, that the enemy are daily gathering strength from the disaffected. This strength, like a snow-ball by rolling, will increase unless some means can be devised to check effectually the progress of the enemy's arms. Militia may possibly do it for a little while; but in a little while, also, and the militia of those States, which have been frequently called upon, will not turn out at all; or, if they do, it will be with so much reluctance and sloth, as to amount to the same thing. Instance New Jersey! Witness Pennsylvania! Could anything but the river Delaware have saved Philadelphia? Can anything (the exigency of the case indeed may justify it) be more destructive to the recruiting service, than giving ten dollars' bounty for six weeks' service of the militia, who come in, you cannot tell how, go, you cannot tell when, and act, you cannot tell where, consume your provisions, exhaust your stores, and leave you at last at a critical moment?

These, Sir, are the men I am to depend upon, ten days hence; this is the basis, on which your cause will and must forever depend, till you get a large standing army sufficient of itself to oppose the enemy. I therefore beg leave to give it as my humble opinion, that eighty-eight battalions are by no means equal to the opposition you are to make, and that a moment's time is not to be lost in raising a greater number, not less, in my opinion and the opinion of my officers, than a hundred and ten. It may be urged that it will be found difficult enough to complete the first number. This may be true, and yet the officers of a hundred and ten battalions will recruit many more men, than those of eighty-eight. In my judgment this is not a time to stand upon expense; our funds are not the only object of consideration. The State of New York have added one battalion (I wish they had made it two) to their quota. If any good officers will offer to raise men upon Continental pay and establishment in this quarter, I shall encourage them to do so, and regiment them when they have done it. If Congress disapprove of this proceeding, they will please to signify it, as I mean it for the best. It may be thought that I am going a good deal out of the line of my duty, to adopt these measures, or to advise thus freely. A character to lose, an estate to forfeit, the inestimable blessing of liberty at stake, and a life devoted, must be my excuse.

# THE BATTLES OF TRENTON AND PRINCETON

*By General George Washington*

*IT WAS to fight the battle of Trenton, in New Jersey, December 26, 1776, that Washington at the head of 2,400 men made his famous crossing of the ice-jammed Delaware River. He surprised the Hessians under Colonel Rahl and took more than 1,000 prisoners, paving the way for the equally important victory over the British at Princeton on January third following.*

*Frederick the Great esteemed this Trenton-Princeton campaign "the most brilliant military performance of the century"; and Cornwallis himself, at a banquet given him and his staff by Washington after the surrender at Yorktown, declared that when history's verdict was made up "the brightest garlands for your Excellency will be gathered, not from the shores of the Chesapeake, but from the banks of the Delaware."*

*These are the military reports sent by Washington to John Hancock as President of Congress shortly after the respective battles were fought.*

I HAVE the pleasure of congratulating you upon the success of an enterprise, which I had formed against a detachment of the enemy lying at Trenton, and which was executed yesterday morning. The evening of the twenty-fifth I ordered the troops intended for this service to parade back to McKonkey's Ferry, that they might begin to pass as soon as it grew dark, imagining we should be able to throw them all over, with the necessary artillery, by twelve o'clock, and that we might easily arrive at Trenton by five in the morning, the distance being about nine miles. But the quantity of ice, made that night, impeded the passage of the boats so much, that it was three o'clock before the artillery could all be got over; and

near four before the troops took up their line of
march. This made me despair of surprising the town,
as I well knew we could not reach it before the day
was fairly broke. But as I was certain there was no
making a retreat without being discovered and
harassed on repassing the river, I determined to push
on at all events. I formed my detachment into two
divisions, one to march by the lower or river road, the
other by the upper or Pennington road. As the divisions had nearly the same distance to march, I
ordered each of them, immediately upon forcing the
out-guards, to push directly into the town, that they
might charge the enemy before they had time to form.

The upper division arrived at the enemy's advanced
posts exactly at eight o'clock; and in three minutes
after, I found, from the fire on the lower road, that
the divisions had also got up. The out-guards made
but small opposition, though, for their numbers, they
behaved very well, keeping up a constant retreating
fire from behind houses. We presently saw their
main body formed; but, from their motions, they
seemed undetermined how to act. Being hard
pressed by our troops, who had already got possession
of their artillery, they attempted to file off by a road
on their right, leading to Princeton. But, perceiving
their intention, I threw a body of troops in their way,
which immediately checked them. Finding from our
disposition, that they were surrounded, and that they
must inevitably be cut to pieces if they made any
further resistance, they agreed to lay down their

arms. The number that submitted in this manner was twenty-three officers and eight hundred and eighty-six men. Colonel Rahl, the commanding officer, and seven others were found wounded in the town. I do not exactly know how many were killed; but I fancy twenty or thirty, as they never made any regular stand. Our loss is very trifling indeed, only two officers and one or two privates wounded.

In justice to the officers and men, I must add, that their behavior upon this occasion reflects the highest honor upon them. The difficulty of passing the river in a very severe night, and their march through a violent storm of snow and hail, did not in the least abate their ardor; but, when they came to the charge, each seemed to vie with the other in pressing forward; and were I to give a preference to any particular corps, I should do great injustice to the others.

## ON TO PRINCETON

I HAVE the honor to inform you, that, since the date of my last from Trenton, I have removed with the army under my command to this place. The difficulty of crossing the Delaware, on account of the ice, made our passage over it tedious, and gave the enemy an opportunity of drawing in their several cantonments, and assembling their whole force at Princeton. Their large pickets advanced towards Trenton, their great preparations, and some intelligence I had received, added to their knowledge, that the 1st of

January brought on a dissolution of the best part of our army, gave me the strongest reasons to conclude, that an attack upon us was meditating.

Our situations was most critical, and our force small. . . . On the 2d [of January, 1777], according to my expectation, the enemy began to advance upon us; and, after some skirmishing, the head of their column reached Trenton about four o'clock, whilst their rear was as far back as Maidenhead. They attempted to pass Sanpink Creek, which runs through Trenton, at different places; but, finding the forts guarded, they halted, and kindled their fires. We were drawn up on the other side of the creek. In this situation we remained till dark, cannonading the enemy, and receiving the fire of their field-pieces, which did us but little damage.

Having by this time discovered that the enemy were greatly superior in number, and that their design was to surround us, I ordered all our baggage to be removed silently to Burlington soon after dark; and at twelve o'clock after renewing our fires, and leaving guards at the bridge in Trenton, and other passes on the same stream above, marched by a roundabout road to Princeton, where I knew they could not have much force left, and might have stores. One thing I was certain of, that it would avoid the appearance of a retreat (which was of consequence, or to run the hazard of the whole army being cut off), whilst we might by a fortunate stroke withdraw General Howe from Trenton, and give some reputation to our arms.

Happily we succeeded.  We found Princeton about sunrise, with only three regiments and three troops of light-horse in it, two of which were on their march to Trenton.  These three regiments, especially the two first, made a gallant resistance, and, in killed, wounded, and prisoners, must have lost five hundred men; upwards of one hundred of them were left dead on the field; and, with what I have with me and what were taken in the pursuit and carried across the Delaware, there are near three hundred prisoners, fourteen of whom are officers, all British. . . .

. . . We took two brass field-pieces; but, for want of horses, could not bring them away.  We also took some blankets, shoes, and a few other trifling articles, burned the hay, and destroyed such other things, as the shortness of the time would admit of. . . .

. . . The militia are taking spirits, and, I am told, are coming in fast from this State [New Jersey]; but I fear those from Philadelphia will scarcely submit to the hardships of a winter campaign much longer, especially as they very unluckily sent their blankets with their baggage to Burlington.  I must do them the justice however to add, that they have undergone more fatigue and hardship, than I expected militia, especially citizens, would have done at this inclement season.  I am just moving to Morristown, where I shall endeavor to put them under the best cover I can.  Hitherto we have been without any; and many of our poor soldiers quite barefoot, and ill clad in other respects. . . .

# THE DEFEAT AND SURRENDER OF BURGOYNE

*By Frederika Charlotte Louise, Baroness von Riedesel*

*THIS article is from the "Letters and Journals" of Baroness von Riedesel, whose husband commanded the German troops in Burgoyne's army at the Battle of Saratoga, October 9, 1777. After the surrender to General Gates, both General Riedesel and his wife were prisoners for nearly three years. They were exchanged in 1780 and Riedesel was given command of the British forces on Long Island, his wife accompanying him.*

*Burgoyne with 11,000 men was marching south from Canada to join forces with General Howe. A dispatch directing General Howe to proceed up the Hudson had been written, but Lord North in his haste to leave London for a holiday did not sign it. It was pigeon-holed and not found until it turned up years later in the British army archives. But for this inadvertence, the battle of Saratoga might have been a British victory.*

WE were halted at six o'clock in the morning [October 9, 1777], to our general amazement. General Burgoyne ordered the artillery to be drawn up in a line, and to have it counted. This gave much dissatisfaction, as a few marches more would have ensured our safety. My husband was exhausted by fatigue, and took a seat in the calash, where my maids made room for him; and he slept for three hours upon my shoulder. In the meantime, Captain Willoe brought me his pocket-book, containing bank-notes, and Captain Geismar, a beautiful watch, a ring, and a well-provided purse, requesting me to keep them, which I promised to do to the last. At length we recommenced our march; but scarcely an hour had elapsed, before the army was again halted, because the enemy was in sight. They were but two hundred in number, who came to reconnoitre, and who might easily have been taken, had not General Burgoyne lost all his presence of mind. The rain fell in torrents. . . . On the 9th, it rained terribly the whole day; nevertheless we kept ourselves ready to march. The savages had lost their courage, and they walked off in all directions. The least untoward event made them dispirited, especially when there was no opportunity for plunder. My chamber-maid exclaimed the whole day against her fate, and seemed mad with despair. I begged her to be quiet, unless she wished to be taken for a savage. Upon this she became still more extravagant, and asked me, "If I should be sorry for it?"—"Surely," replied I.—She then tore her cap from her head, and let her hair fall upon her face. "You take it quite easily," said she, "for you have your husband; but we have nothing but the prospect of being killed, or of losing the little we possess." . . .

We reached Saratoga about dark, which was but half an hour's march from the place where we had spent the day. I was quite wet, and was obliged to remain in that condition, for want of a place to change my apparel. I seated myself near the fire, and undressed the children, and we then laid ourselves upon some straw.—I asked General Phillips, who came to see how I was, why we did not continue our retreat, my husband having pledged himself to cover the movement, and to bring off the army in safety. "My poor lady," said he, "you astonish me. Though quite wet, you have so much courage as to wish to go farther in this weather. What a pity it is that you are not our commanding general! He complains of fatigue, and has determined upon spending the night here, and giving us a supper."

It is very true, that General Burgoyne liked to make himself easy, and that he spent half his nights in singing and drinking, and diverting himself. . . . I refreshed myself at 7 o'clock, the next morning, (the 10th of October,) with a cup of tea, and we all expected that we should soon continue our march. . . . About 2 o'clock, we heard again a report of muskets and cannon, and there was much alarm and bustle among our troops. My husband sent me word, that I should immediately retire into a house which was not far off. I got into my calash with my children, and when we were near the house, I saw, on the opposite bank of the Hudson, five or six men, who aimed at us with their guns. Without knowing what I did, I threw my children into the back part of the vehicle, and laid myself upon them. At the same moment the fellow fired, and broke the arm of a poor English soldier, who stood behind us, and who being already wounded sought a shelter. Soon after our arrival, a terrible cannonade began, and the fire was principally directed against the house, where we had hoped to find a refuge, probably because the enemy inferred, from the great number of people who went towards it, that this was the headquarters of the generals, while, in reality, none were there except women and crippled soldiers. We were at last obliged to descend into the cellar, where I laid myself in a corner near the door. My children put their heads upon my knees. An abominable smell, the cries of the children, and my own anguish of mind, did not permit me to close my eyes, during the whole night. On the next morning, the cannonade begun anew, but in a different direction. . . . Eleven cannon-balls passed through the house, and made a tremendous noise. A poor soldier, who was about to have a leg amputated, lost the other by one of these balls. All his comrades ran away at that moment, and when they returned, they found him in one corner of the room, in the agonies of death. I was myself in the deepest distress, not so much on account of my own dangers, as of those to which my husband was exposed, who, however, frequently sent me messages, inquiring after my health. . . .

The want of water continuing to distress us, we could not but be extremely glad to find a soldier's wife so spirited as to fetch some from the river, an occupation from which the boldest might have shrunk, as the Americans shot every one who approached it. They told us afterwards that they spared her on account of her sex. . . .

On the 17th of October, the capitulation was carried into effect. The generals waited upon the American General Gates, and the troops surrendered

themselves prisoners of war and laid down their arms.
The time had now come for the good woman who
had risked her life to supply us with water, to receive
the reward of her services. Each of us threw a handful of money into her apron; and she thus received
more than twenty guineas. At such a moment at
least, if at no other, the heart easily overflows with
gratitude.

At last, my husband's groom brought me a message to join him with the children. I once more seated
myself in my dear calash, and, while riding through
the American camp, was gratified to observe that no-
body looked at us with disrespect, but, on the contrary, greeted us, and seemed touched at the sight of
a captive mother with three children. I must candidly
confess that I did not present myself, though so situated, with much courage to the enemy, for the thing
was entirely new to me. When I drew near the tents,
a good looking man advanced towards me, and helped
the children from the calash, and kissed and caressed
them: he then offered me his arms, and tears trembled
in his eyes. "You tremble," said he; "do not be
alarmed, I pray you." "Sir," cried I, "a countenance
so expressive of benevolence, and the kindness which
you have evinced towards my children, are sufficient
to dispel all apprehension." He then ushered me into
the tent of General Gates. . . .

. . . The gentleman who had received me with so
much kindness, came and said to me, "You may find
it embarrassing to be the only lady in such a large

company of gentlemen; will you come with your children to my tent, and partake of a frugal dinner, offered with the best will?" "By the kindness you show to me," returned I, "you induce me to believe that you have a wife and children." He informed me that he was General Schuyler. He regaled me with smoked tongues, which were excellent, with beefsteaks, potatoes, fresh butter, and bread. Never did a dinner give me so much pleasure as this. I was easy, after many months of anxiety, and I read the same happy change in the countenances of those around me. . . .

# LAFAYETTE ARRIVES IN AMERICA

*He Records His Early Impressions*

GENERAL Marie Paul Joseph, Marquis de Lafayette, to give the distinguished French patriot and friend of Washington his full name, was less than twenty years of age when he landed at Georgetown, South Carolina, en route to Philadelphia to offer his military services to Congress. In view of his youth, it may surprise the reader of the accompanying letter to his wife, dated Charleston, June 19, 1777, to find him sending love to their children. However, Lafayette had married at the age of seventeen.

Seized with enthusiasm for the cause of the American colonists, along with admiration for Washington, he fitted out a ship in disobedience to the French Government, and, sailing from Pasages, in Spain, arrived in America with eleven companions, among them Baron de Kalb. His presence did much to give new hope to supporters of the Revolutionary cause at a time when they were most discouraged.

MY last letter to you, my dear love, has informed you, that I arrived safely in this country, after having suffered a little from seasickness during the first weeks of the voyage; that I was then, the morning after I landed, at the house of a very kind officer; that I had been nearly two months on the passage, and that I wished to set off immediately. It spoke of everything most interesting to my heart; of my sorrow at parting from you, and of our dear children; and it said, besides, that I was in excellent health. I give you this abstract of it, because the English may possibly amuse themselves by seizing it on its way. I have such confidence in my lucky star, however, that I hope it will reach you. This same star has befriended me, to the astonishment of everybody here. Trust to it yourself, and be assured that it ought to calm all your fears. I landed after having sailed several days along a coast, which swarmed with hostile vessels. When I arrived, everybody said that my vessel must inevitably be taken, since two British frigates blockaded the harbor. I even went so far as to send orders to the captain, both by land and sea, to put the men on shore and set fire to the ship, if not yet too late. By a most wonderful good fortune, a gale obliged the frigates to stand out to sea for a short time. My vessel came in at noon-day, without meeting friend or foe.

At Charleston I have met General Howe, an American officer now in the service. The Governor of the State is expected this evening from the country. All with whom I wished to become acquainted here, have shown me the greatest politeness and attention. I feel entirely satisfied with my reception, although I have not thought it best to go into any detail respecting my arrangements and plans. I wish first to see Congress. I hope to set out for Philadelphia in two days. Our route is more than two hundred and fifty leagues by land. We shall divide ourselves into small parties. I have already purchased horses and light carriages for the journey. Some French and American vessels are here, and are to sail together to-morrow morning, taking advantage of a moment when the frigates are out of sight. They are armed, and have promised me to defend themselves stoutly

against the small privateers, which they will certainly
meet.  I shall distribute my letters among the different
ships.

I will now tell you about the country and its inhabitants.  They are as agreeable as my enthusiasm had
painted them.  Simplicity of manners, kindness, love
of country and of liberty, and a delightful equality
everywhere prevail.  The wealthiest man and the
poorest are on a level; and, although there are some
large fortunes, I challenge any one to discover the
slightest difference between the manners of these two
classes respectively towards each other.  I first saw
the country life at the house of Major Huger.  I am
now in the city, where everything is very much after
the English fashion, except that there is more simplicity, equality, cordiality, and courtesy here than
in England.  The city of Charleston is one of the
handsomest and best built, and its inhabitants among
the most agreeable, that I have ever seen.  The American women are very pretty, simple in their manners,
and exhibit a neatness, which is everywhere cultivated
even more studiously than in England.  What most
charms me is, that all the citizens are brethren.  In
America, there are no poor, nor even what we call
peasantry.  Each individual has his own honest property, and the same rights as the most wealthy landed
proprietor.  The inns are very different from those
of Europe; the host and hostess sit at table with you,
and do the honors of a comfortable meal; and, on
going away, you pay your bill without higgling.

When one does not wish to go to an inn, there are country-houses where the title of a good American is a sufficient passport to all those civilities paid in Europe to one's friend.

As to my own reception, it has been most agreeable in every quarter; and to have come with me secures the most flattering welcome. I have just passed five hours at a grand dinner, given in honor of me by an individual of this city. Generals Howe and Moultrie, and several officers of my suite, were present. We drank healths and tried to talk English. I begin to speak it a little. To-morrow I shall go with these gentlemen to call on the Governor of the State, and make arrangements for my departure. The next day the commanding officers here will show me the city and its environs, and then I shall set out for the army.

Considering the pleasant life I lead in this country, my sympathy with the people, which makes me feel as much at ease in their society as if I had known them for twenty years, the similarity between their mode of thinking and my own, and my love of liberty and of glory, one might suppose that I am very happy. But you are not with me; my friends are not with me; and there is no happiness for me far from you and them. I ask you, if you still love me; but I put the same question much oftener to myself, and my heart always responds, Yes. I am impatient beyond measure to hear from you. I hope to find letters at Philadelphia. My only fear is, that the privateer, which is to bring them, may be captured on her passage. Although I suppose I have drawn upon me the special displeasure of the English, by taking the liberty to depart in spite of them, and by landing in their very face, yet I confess they will not be in arrears with me, should they capture this vessel, my cherished hope, on which I so fondly depend for letters from you. Write frequent and long letters. You do not know the full extent of the joy with which I shall receive them. Embrace Henrietta tenderly. May I say embrace tenderly our children? The father of these poor children is a rover, but a good and honest man at heart; a good father, who loves his family dearly, and a good husband, who loves his wife with all his heart.

Remember me to your friends and my own, to the dear society, once the society of the court, but which by the lapse of time has become the society of the Wooden Sword. We republicans think it all the better. I must leave off for want of paper and time; and if I do not repeat to you ten thousand times that I love you, it is not from any want of feeling, but from modesty; since I have the presumption to hope, that I have already convinced you of it. The night is far advanced, and the heat dreadful. I am devoured by insects; so, you see, the best countries have their disadvantages. Adieu.

# LAFAYETTE IN THE AMERICAN REVOLUTION

*From Lafayette's Memoirs*

*THIS account of his first visit to America and of his military service on Washington's staff is much the fullest and most important part of the "Memoirs, Correspondence and Manuscripts of General Lafayette," published by his family. Under the head of the American Revolution are comprised eight years of his life, from the beginning of 1777 until the end of 1784, the latter being his twenty-eighth year of age.*

*On the breaking out of the war between France and England, Lafayette returned home (January, 1779) and it was largely through his exertions that the French government dispatched a land force as well as a fleet to the aid of the Americans.*

*Returning to his command in 1781, Lafayette was hotly engaged by Cornwallis in Virginia. Once Cornwallis exulted, "The boy cannot escape me." Not many weeks later he surrendered, and Lafayette was publicly thanked by Washington.*

*In the middle of the article Lafayette changes from the first to the third person in this account.*

YOU ask me at what period I first experienced my ardent love of liberty and glory? I recollect no time of my life anterior to my enthusiasm for anecdotes of glorious deeds, and to my projects of travelling over the world to acquire fame. At eight years of age, my heart beat when I heard of an hyæna that had done some injury, and caused still more alarm, in our neighborhood, and the hope of meeting it was the object of all my walks. When I arrived at college, nothing ever interrupted my studies, except my ardent wish of studying without restraint. I never deserved to be chastised, but, in spite of my usual gentleness, it would have been dangerous to have attempted to do so; and I recollect with pleasure that, when I was to describe in

222

rhetoric a perfect courser, I sacrificed the hope of obtaining a premium, and described the one who, on perceiving the whip, threw down his rider. Republican anecdotes always delighted me; and, when my new connections wished to obtain for me a place at court, I did not hesitate displeasing them to preserve my independence. I was in that frame of mind when I first learnt the troubles in America: they only became thoroughly known in Europe in 1776, and the memorable declaration of the 4th of July reached France at the close of that same year.

After having crowned herself with laurels and enriched herself with conquests, after having become mistress of all seas, and after having insulted all nations, England had turned her pride against her own colonies. North America had long been displeasing to her: she wished to add new vexations to former injuries, and to destroy the most sacred privileges. . . .

(1776.) When I first learnt the subject of this quarrel, my heart espoused warmly the cause of liberty, and I thought of nothing but of adding also the aid of my banner. Some circumstances, which it would be needless to relate, had taught me to expect only obstacles in this case from my own family: I depended, therefore, solely upon myself; and I ventured to adopt for a device on my arms these words,— "Cur non?"—that they might equally serve as an encouragement to myself, and as a reply to others. Silas Deane was then at Paris; but the ministers feared to receive him, and his voice was overpowered by the louder accents of Lord Stormont. He despatched privately to America some old arms, which were of little use, and some young officers, who did but little good, the whole directed by M. de Beaumarchais; and, when the English ambassador spoke to our court, it denied having sent any cargoes, ordered those that were preparing to be discharged, and dismissed from our ports all American privateers. While wishing to address myself in a direct manner to Mr. Deane, I became the friend of Kalb, a German in our employ, who was applying for service with the insurgents (the expression in use at that time), and who became my interpreter. He was the person sent by M. de Choiseul to examine the English colonies; and on his return he received some money, but never succeeded in obtaining an audience, so little did that minister in reality think of the revolution whose retrograde movements some persons have inscribed to him! When I presented to Mr. Deane my boyish face (for I was scarcely nineteen years of age), I spoke more of my ardor in the cause than of my experience; but I dwelt much upon the effect my departure would excite in France, and he signed our mutual agreement. . . .

Preparations were making to send a vessel to America, when very bad tidings arrived from thence. New York, Long Island, White Plains, Fort Washington, and the Jerseys had seen the American forces successively destroyed by thirty-three thousand Englishmen or Germans. Three thousand Americans alone remained in arms, and these were closely pursued by General Howe. From that moment all the credit of the insurgents vanished: to obtain a vessel for them was impossible. The envoys themselves thought it right to express to me their own discouragement, and persuade me to abandon my project. I called upon Mr. Deane, and I thanked him for his frankness. "Until now, sir," said I, "you have only seen my ardor in your cause, and that may not prove at present wholly useless. I shall purchase a ship to carry out your officers. We must feel confidence in the future, and it is especially in the hour of danger that I wish to share your fortune." My project was received with approbation; but it was necessary afterwards to find money, and to purchase and arm a vessel secretly: all this was accomplished with the greatest despatch.

The period was, however, approaching, which had been long fixed, for my taking a journey to England. I could not refuse to go without risking the discovery of my secret, and by consenting to take this journey I knew I could better conceal my preparations for a greater one. This last measure was also thought most expedient by MM. Franklin and Deane, for the doctor himself was then in France; and, although I did not venture to go to his home, for fear of being seen, I corresponded with him through M. Carmichael, an American less generally known. I arrived in London with M. de Poix; and I first paid my respects to Bancroft, the American, and afterwards to his British Majesty. . . .

After having suffered dreadfully in the Channel, and being reminded, as a consolation, how very short the voyage would be, I arrived at M. de Kalb's house in Paris, concealed myself three days at Chaillot, saw a few of my friends and some Americans, and set out for Bordeaux, where I was for some time unexpectedly delayed. I took advantage of that delay to send to Paris, from whence the intelligence I received was by no means encouraging; but, as my messenger was followed on his road by one from the government, I lost not a moment in setting sail, and the orders of my sovereign were only able to overtake me at Pasage, a Spanish port, at which we stopped on our way. The letters from my own family were extremely violent, and those from the government were peremptory. I was forbidden to proceed to the American continent under the penalty of disobedience; I was enjoined to repair instantly to Marseilles, and await there further orders. A sufficient number of commentaries were not wanting upon the consequences of such an anathema, the laws of the state, and the power and displeasure of the government; but the grief of his wife, who was pregnant, and the thoughts of his family and friends, had far more effect upon M. de Lafayette. As his vessel could no longer be stopped, he returned to Bordeaux to enter into a justification of his own conduct; and, in a declaration to M. de Fumel, he took upon himself all the consequences of his present evasion. As the court did not deign to relax in its determination, he wrote to M. de

Maurepas that that silence was a tacit consent, and his own departure took place soon after that joking despatch. After having set out on the road to Marseilles, he retraced his steps, and, disguised as a courier, he had almost escaped all danger, when, at Saint Jean de Luz, a young girl recognized him; but a sign from him silenced her, and her adroit fidelity turned away all suspicion. It was then that M. de Lafayette rejoined his ship, the 26th of April, 1777; and on that same day, after six months' anxiety and labor, he set sail for the American continent.

(1777.) As soon as M. de Lafayette had recovered from the effects of sea-sickness, he studied the language and trade he was adopting. A heavy ship, two bad cannons, and some guns could not have escaped from the smallest privateer. In his present situation, he resolved rather to blow up the vessel than to surrender. He concerted measures to achieve this end with a brave Dutchman named Bedaulx, whose sole alternative, if taken, would have been the gibbet. The captain insisted upon stopping at the islands; but government orders would have been found there, and he followed a direct course, less from choice than from compulsion. At forty leagues from shore, they were met by a small vessel. The captain turned pale, but the crew were attached to M. de Lafayette, and the officers were numerous: they made a show of resistance. It turned out, fortunately, to be an American ship, whom they vainly endeavored to keep up with; but scarcely had the former lost sight of M. de

Lafayette's vessel, when it fell in with two English frigates,—and this is not the only time when the elements seemed bent on opposing M. de Lafayette, as if with the intention of saving him. After having encountered for seven weeks various perils and chances, he arrived at Georgetown, in Carolina. Ascending the river in a canoe, his foot touched at length the American soil; and he swore that he would conquer or perish in that cause. Landing at midnight at Major Huger's house, he found a vessel sailing for France, which appeared only waiting for his letters. Several of the officers landed, others remained on board, and all hastened to proceed to Charlestown. . . .

To repair to the Congress of the United States, M. de Lafayette rode nearly nine hundred miles on horseback. Before reaching the capital of Pennsylvania, he was obliged to travel through the two Carolinas, Virginia, Maryland, and Delaware. While studying the language and customs of the inhabitants, he observed also new productions of nature and new methods of cultivation. Vast forests and immense rivers combine to give to that country an appearance of youth and majesty. After a fatiguing journey of one month he beheld at length that Philadelphia, so well known in the present day, and whose future grandeur Penn appeared to designate when he laid the first stone of its foundation.

After having accomplished his noble manœuvres at Trenton and Princeton, General Washington had remained in his camp at Middlebrook. The English, finding themselves frustrated in their first hopes, combined to make a decisive campaign. Burgoyne was already advancing with ten thousand men, preceded by his proclamation and his savages. Ticonderoga, a famous stand of arms, was abandoned by Saint-Clair. He drew upon himself much public odium by this deed, but he saved the only corps whom the militia could rally around. Whilst the generals were busied assembling that militia, the Congress recalled them, sent Gates in their place, and used all possible means to support him. At that same time the great English army, of about eighteen thousand men, had sailed from New York, and the two Howes were uniting their forces for a secret enterprise. Rhode Island was occupied by an hostile corps; and General Clinton, who had remained at New York, was there preparing for an expedition. To be able to withstand so many various blows, General Washington, leaving Putnam on the North river, crossed over the Delaware, and encamped, with eleven thousand men, within reach of Philadelphia.

It was under these circumstances that M. de Lafayette first arrived in America; but the moment, although important to the common cause, was peculiarly unfavorable to strangers. The Americans were displeased with the pretensions, and disgusted with the conduct, of many Frenchmen. The imprudent selections they had in some cases made, the extreme boldness of some foreign adventurers, the jealousy of the army, and strong national prejudices, all contributed to confound disinterested zeal with private ambition, and talents with quackery. Supported by the promises which had been given by Mr. Deane, a numerous band of foreigners besieged the Congress. Their chief was a clever but very imprudent man; and, although a good officer, his excessive vanity amounted almost to madness. With M. de Lafayette, Mr. Deane had sent out a fresh detachment; and every day such crowds arrived that the Congress had finally adopted the plan of not listening to any stranger. The coldness with which M. de Lafayette was received might have been taken as a dismissal; but, without appearing disconcerted by the manner in which the deputies addressed him, he entreated them to return to Congress, and read the following note:—

"After the sacrifices I have made, I have the right to exact two favors: one is, to serve at my own expense; the other is, to serve at first as volunteer."

This style, to which they were so little accustomed, awakened their attention: the despatches from the envoys were read over; and, in a very flattering resolution, the rank of major-general was granted to M. de Lafayette. . . .

The two Howes having appeared before the capes of the Delaware, General Washington came to Philadelphia, and M. de Lafayette beheld for the first time that great man. Although he was surrounded by officers and citizens, it was impossible to mistake for a moment his majestic figure and deportment; nor was he less distinguished by the noble affability of his manner. M. de Lafayette accompanied him in his examination of the fortifications. Invited by the General to establish himself in his house, he looked upon it from that moment as his own: with this perfect ease and simplicity was formed the tie that united two friends, whose confidence and attachment were to be cemented by the strongest interests of humanity. . . .

After having menaced the Delaware, the English fleet again disappeared, and during some days the Americans amused themselves by making jokes at its expense. These jokes, however, ceased when it reappeared in the Chesapeake; and, in order to approach it more closely during the disembarkation, the patriot army crossed through the town. Their heads covered with green branches, and marching to the sound of drums and fifes, these soldiers, in spite of their state of nudity, offered an agreeable spectacle to the eyes of all the citizens. General Washington was marching at their head, and M. de Lafayette was by his side. The army stationed itself upon the heights of Wilmington, and that of the enemy landed in the Elk River, at the bottom of Chesapeake bay. . . .

After having advanced as far as Wilmington, the General had detached a thousand men under Maxwell, the most ancient brigadier in the army. At the first march of the English, he was beaten by their advance-guard near Christiana Bridge. During that time the army took but an indifferent station at Newport. They then removed a little south, waited two days for the enemy, and, at the moment when these were marching upon their right wing, a nocturnal council of war decided that the army was to proceed to the Brandywine. The stream bearing that name covered its front. The ford called Chad's Ford, placed nearly in the center, was defended by batteries. It was in that hardly examined station that, in obedience to a letter from Congress, the Americans awaited the battle. . . . M. de Lafayette, as volunteer, had always accompanied the General. The left wing remaining in a state of tranquillity, and the right appearing fated to receive all the heavy blows, he obtained permission to join Sullivan. At his arrival, which seemed to inspirit the troops, he found that, the enemy having crossed the ford, the corps of Sullivan had scarcely had time to form itself on a line in front of a thinly wooded forest. A few moments after, Lord Cornwallis formed in the finest order. Advancing across the plain, his first line opened a brisk fire of musketry and artillery. The Americans returned the fire, and did much injury to the enemy; but, their right and left wings having given way, the generals and several officers joined the central division, in which were M. de Lafayette and Stirling, and of which eight hundred men were commanded in a most brilliant manner by Conway, an Irishman, in the service of France. By separating that division from its two wings, and advancing through an open plain, in which they lost many men, the enemy united all his fire upon the center: the confusion became extreme; and it was while M. de Lafayette was rallying the troops that a ball passed through his leg. At that moment all those remaining on the field gave way. M. de Lafayette was indebted to Gimat, his aide-de-camp, for the happiness of getting upon his horse. General Washington arrived from a distance with fresh troops. M. de Lafayette was preparing to join him, when loss of blood obliged him to stop and have his wound bandaged: he was even very near being taken. Fugitives, cannon, and baggage now crowded without order into the road leading to Chester. The General employed the remaining daylight in checking the enemy: some regiments behaved extremely well, but the disorder was complete. During that time the ford of Chad was forced, the cannon taken, and the Chester road became the common retreat of the whole army. In the midst of that dreadful confusion, and during the darkness of the night, it was impossible to recover; but at Chester, twelve miles from the field of battle, they met with a bridge which it was necessary to cross. M. de Lafayette occupied himself in arresting the fugitives. Some degree of order was re-established; the generals and the Commander-in-Chief arrived; and he had leisure to have his wound dressed.

It was thus, at twenty-six miles from Philadelphia, that the fate of that town was decided (11th September, 1777). The inhabitants had heard every cannon that was fired there. The two parties, assembled in two distinct bands in all the squares and public places, had awaited the event in silence. The last courier at length arrived, and the friends of liberty were thrown into consternation. The Americans had lost from 1,000 to 1,200 men. Howe's army was composed of about 12,000 men. Their losses had been so considerable that their surgeons, and those in the country, were found insufficient; and they requested the American army to supply them with some for their prisoners. If the enemy had marched to Derby, the army would have been cut up and destroyed. They lost an all-important night; and this was perhaps their greatest fault during a war in which they committed so many errors. . . .

In spite of the Declaration of Independence of the New States, everything there bore the appearance of a civil war. The names of Whig and Tory distinguished the republicans and royalists; the English army was still called the regular troops; the British sovereign was always designated by the name of the king. Provinces, towns, and families were divided by the violence of party spirit: brothers, officers in the two opposing armies, meeting by chance in their father's house, have seized their arms to fight with each other. While in all the rancor of their pride, the English committed horrible acts of license and cruelty, while discipline dragged in her train those venal Germans who knew only how to kill, burn and pillage, in that same army were seen regiments of Americans, who, trampling under foot their brethren, assisted in enslaving their wasted country. . . .

# WASHINGTON AT VALLEY FORGE

*Conditions Described by Doctor Albigence Waldo*

DR. WALDO was a surgeon from Connecticut, of Puritan ancestry, who had volunteered his services to General Washington in the Fall of 1777 and remained throughout that memorable winter with the army at Valley Forge. This is perhaps the best account of the heroism displayed in the darkest period of American affairs, before the French alliance assured money, ships and troops in aid of the Revolution. It is part of a daily diary kept by Dr. Waldo during his military service, beginning on December 12, 1777.

Washington chose Valley Forge as winter quarters for his army partly for its defensibility and partly to protect Congress, then in session at York, Pa., from a sudden British attack. It was here that Baron Steuben trained, disciplined and reorganized the American army, enabling it to fight with greater efficiency in subsequent campaigns, and it was here (May 1, 1778) that news reached Washington of the French alliance.

A BRIDGE of wagons made across the Schuylkill last night consisting of 36 wagons, with a bridge of rails between each. Some skirmishing over the river. Militia and dragoons brought into camp several prisoners. Sunset. We are ordered to march over the river. It snows. I'm sick; eat nothing— no whiskey—no baggage — Lord — Lord — Lord! The army was until sunrise crossing the river— some at the wagon bridge, and some at the raft bridge below. Cold and uncomfortable.

Dec. 13th.—The army marched three miles from the west side of the river and encamped near a place called the Gulf, and not an improper name either; for this Gulf seems well adapted by its situation to keep us from the pleasure and enjoyments of this world, or being conversant with anybody in it. It is an excellent place to raise the ideas of a philosopher beyond the glutted thoughts and reflections of an Epicurean. His reflections will be as different from the common reflections of mankind as if he were unconnected with the world, and only conversant with material beings. It cannot be that our superiors are about to hold consultation with Spirits infinitely beneath their Order—by bringing us into these utmost regions of the terraqueous sphere. No—it is, upon consideration, for many good purposes since we are to winter here—1st. There is plenty of wood and water. 2dly. There are but few families for the soldiery to steal from—though far be it from a soldier to steal—3rdly. There are warm sides of hills to erect huts on. 4thly. They will be heavenly minded like Jonah when in the belly of a great fish. 6thly. They will not become homesick as is sometimes the case when men live in the open world—since the reflections which must naturally arise from their present habitation, will lead them to the more noble thoughts of employing their leisure hours in filling their knapsacks with such materials as may be necessary on the journey to another home.

Dec. 14th.—Prisoners and deserters are continually coming in. The army who have been surprisingly healthy hitherto—now begin to grow sickly from the continued fatigues they have suffered this campaign. Yet they still show spirit of alacrity and contentment

not to be expected from so young troops. I am sick
—discontented—and out of humor. Poor food—
hard lodging—cold weather—fatigue—nasty clothes
—nasty cookery—vomit half my time—smoked out
of my senses—the Devil's in't—I can't endure it—
Why are we sent here to starve and freeze—What
sweet felicities have I left at home;—A charming
wife—pretty children—good beds—good food—good
cookery—all agreeable—all harmonious. Here, all
confusion—smoke cold—hunger and filthiness. A
pox on my bad luck! Here comes a bowl of beef soup
—full of burnt leaves and dirt, sickish enough to
make a Hector spew. Away with it, boys—I'll live
like the chameleon upon air. Poh! Poh! cries patience within me—you talk like a fool. Your being
sick covers your mind with a melancholic gloom,
which makes everything about you appear gloomy.
See the poor soldier, when in health—with what
cheerfulness he meets his foes and encounters every
hardship—if barefoot—he labors through the mud
and cold with a song in his mouth extolling War and
Washington—if his food be bad—he eats it notwithstanding with seeming content—blesses God for a
good stomach—and whistles it into digestion. But
harkee patience—a moment—There comes a soldier
—his bare feet are seen through his worn out shoes
—his legs nearly naked from the tattered remains of
an only pair of stockings—his breeches not sufficient
to cover his nakedness—his shirt hanging in strings
—his hair disheveled—his face meager—his whole

appearance pictures a person forsaken and discouraged. He comes, and cries with an air of wretchedness and despair, "I am sick, my feet lame, my legs are sore, my body covered with this tormenting itch, my clothes are worn out, my constitution is broken, my former activity is exhausted by fatigue, hunger and cold. I fail fast, I shall soon be no more! and all the reward I shall get will be, "Poor Will is dead." . . .

Dec. 18th.—Universal Thanksgiving—a roasted pig at night. God be thanked for my health which I have pretty well recovered. How much better should I feel, were I assured my family were in health. But the same good Being who graciously preserves me is able to preserve them—and bring me to the ardently wished for enjoyment of them again.

Rank and precedence make a good deal of disturbance and confusion in the American army. The army are poorly supplied wtih provision, occasioned, it is said, by the neglect of the Commissary of Purchases. Much talk among officers about discharges. Money has become of too little consequence. . . .

Dec. 21st.—Preparations made for huts. Provision scarce. Mr. Ellis went homeward—sent a letter to my wife. Heartily wish myself at home—my skin and eyes are almost spoiled with continual smoke.

A general cry through the camp this evening among the soldiers—"No Meat!—No Meat!"—the distant vales echoed back the melancholy sound—"No Meat! No Meat!" Imitating the noise of crows and owls, also, made a part of the confused music.

What have you for our dinners, boys? "Nothing but fire cake and water, Sir." At night—"Gentlemen, the supper is ready." What is your supper, Lads? "Fire cake and water, Sir."

Dec. 22d.—Lay excessive cold and uncomfortable last night—my eyes are started out from their orbits like a rabbit's eyes, occasioned by a great cold—and smoke.

What have you got for breakfast, lads? "Fire cake and water, Sir." The Lord send that our Commissary of Purchases may live on fire cake and water. . . .

Our Division is under marching orders this morning. I am ashamed to say it, but I am tempted to steal fowls if I could find them—or even a whole hog—for I feel as if I could eat one. But the impoverished country about us, affords but little matter to employ a thief—or keep a clever fellow in good humor. But why do I talk of hunger and hard usage, when so many in the world have not even fire cake and water to eat. . . .

23d.—The party that went out last evening has not returned to-day. This evening an excellent player on the violin in that soft kind of music which is so finely adapted to stir up the tender passions, while he was playing in the next tent to mine these kind soft airs it immediately called up in remembrance all the endearing expressions—the tender sentiments—the sympathetic friendship that has given so much satisfaction and sensible pleasure to me from the first time I gained the heart and affections of the tenderest of the fair. . . .

Dec. 24th.—Party of the 22d returned. Huts go on slowly—cold and smoke make us fret. But mankind are always fretting, even if they have more than their proportion of the blessings of life. We are never easy—always repining at the Providence of an All-wise and Benevolent Being—blaming our country— or faulting our friends. But I don't know of anything that vexes a man's soul more than hot smoke continually blowing into his eyes, and when he attempts to avoid it, is met by a cold and piercing wind. . . .

Dec. 25th, Christmas.—We are still in tents—when we ought to be in huts—the poor sick suffer much in tents this cold weather—But we now treat them differently from what they used to be at home, under the inspection of old women and Dr. Bolus Linctus. We give them mutton and grog—and a capital medicine once in a while—to start the disease from its foundation at once. We avoid—piddling pills, powders, bolus's linctus's, cordials, and all such insignificant matters whose powers are only rendered important by causing the patient to vomit up his money instead of his disease. But very few of the sick men die.

Dec. 26th.—Party of the 22d not returned. The enemy have been some days the west Schuylkill from opposite the city to Derby—Their intentions are not yet known. The city is at present pretty clear of them. Why don't his Excellency rush in and retake the city, in which he will doubtless find much plunder?—Because he knows better than to leave his post and be caught like a . . . fool cooped up in the city. He has always acted wisely hitherto. His conduct when closely scrutinized is uncensurable. Were his inferior Generals as skillful as himself, we should have the grandest choir of officers ever God made. . . .

Dec. 28th.—Yesterday upwards of fifty officers in Gen. Greene's Division resigned their commissions; six or seven of our regiment are doing the like to-day. All this is occasioned by officers' families being so much neglected at home on account of provisions. Their wages will not buy considerable, purchase a few trifling comfortables here in camp, and maintain their families at home, while such extravagant prices are demanded for the common necessaries of life, what then have they to purchase clothes and other necessaries with? It is a melancholy reflection that what is of the most universal importance, is most universally neglected—I mean keeping up the credit of money.

The present circumstances of the soldier is better by far than the officer, for the family of the soldier is provided for at the public expense if the articles they want are above the common price; but the officer's family are obliged not only to beg in the most humble manner for the necessaries of life but also to pay for them afterwards at the most exorbitant rates—and even in this manner, many of them who depend entirely on their money, cannot procure half the material comforts that are wanted in a family. This produces continual letters of complaint from home. . . .

Dec. 31st.—Adjutant Selden learned me how to darn stockings—to make them look like knit work —first work the thread in a parallel manner, then catch these over and over as above. . . .

1778. January 1st.—New Year. I am alive. I am well.

Huts go on briskly, and our camp begins to appear like a spacious city. . . .

Bought an embroidered jacket.

How much we affect to appear of consequence by a superfluous dress,—and yet custom—(that law which none may fight against) has rendered this absolutely necessary and commendable. An officer frequently fails of being duly noticed, merely from the want of a genteel dress. . . .

Sunday, Jan. 4th.—Properly accoutered I went to work at masonry.—None of my Mess were to dictate me, and before night (being found with mortar and stone) I almost completed a genteel chimney to my magnificent hut—however, as we had short allowance of food and no grog—my back ached before night.

I was called to relieve a soldier thought to be dying —he expired before I reached the hut. He was an Indian—an excellent soldier—and an obedient good natured fellow. . . .

8th.—Unexpectedly got a furlough. Set out for home. The very worst of riding—mud and mire.

We had gone through inoculation before this furlough.

| | | | |
|---|---|---|---|
| Lodged at—Porters . . . . . . . | £0 | 12 | 0 |
| Breakfasted at Weaver Jan. 9th just by | | | |
| Bartholomews . . . . . . . . . | 0 | 5 | |
| Grog . . . . . . . . . . . . | 0 | 4 | |
| Hyelyars Tavern 3½ from Caryls, dined | 0 | 5 | 10 |
| Shocking riding! | | | |
| Lodged at a private house three miles this | | | |
| side Delaware in Jersey and Breakfasted | 0 | 6 | 0 |
| Treat Serj. Palmer with Baggage . . . | 0 | 5 | 2 |
| Mattersons Tavern 13 m De War . . . | 0 | 4 | 0 |
| Mattersons . . . . . . . . . . | 0 | 2 | 0 |
| Conarts Tavern 10 M. . . . . . . | 0 | 5 | 0 |
| Sharps or McCurdys, 4 M. . . . . . | 0 | 13 | 0 |
| Capt. Porter's Cross Road 2 M. from Mc- | | | |
| Curdy's Lodged—5 Dol. 1 Sixth . . | 1 | 11 | 0 |
| Breakfasted at the pretty Cottagers Jan. | | | |
| 11th . . . . . . . . . . . | 0 | 5 | 6 |
| 1 M. from Porters—Horses . . . . | | 0 | 0 |
| Lodgings &c. . . . . . . . . . | 0 | 11 | 0 |
| Bullions Tavern (Vealtown) . . . . | 0 | 5 | 0 |
| Morristown Dined . . . . . . . . | 0 | 5 | 0 |
| Poquonnack 10 M. from N. Y. at Jennings | | | |
| Tavern and a narrow bed—Lodged | | | |
| here. Landlady with toothache—Chil- | | | |
| dren keep a squalling . . . . . | 0 | 19 | |
| Roomë's or Romer's Tavern—Good | | | |
| tavern—11 Mile from Jennings . . . | 0 | 20 | 0 |

For 2 bowls Grog and Rum Vaulk's
    house— . . . . . . . . . .£0 10 0
Honey and Bread and Oats . . . . . 0 12
Good old squeaking Widow Ann Hopper,
    26 M. from Jenning's, fine living, for
    horse, Supper, Lodged, Breakfasted . 0 12 0
Satyr Tavern—Lodged and Supped . . 0 9 6
Judge Coe's, 9 M. from King's Ferry Din-
    ner, Oats . . . . . . . . . . 0 6 0

                             £8 19 6

# LETTERS OF LAFAYETTE AND WASHINGTON

TO AN American nothing relating to Lafayette is of more interest than his friendship with Washington. More than a hundred of the letters that passed between the two men are given in Lafayette's Memoirs, and they constitute by far the most interesting and important portion of the correspondence there preserved. The first letters, including the two here printed, belong to the trying time of Conway's Cabal, and show the complete confidence which Washington and Lafayette reposed in each other, despite their wide difference in age.

The story of their enduring friendship, as warm on one side as on the other, written in these letters, is a part of the great history which Washington and Lafayette helped to make in America and in France. The Lafayette letter was dated from his camp December 30, 1777. Washington's reply was dated from his headquarters the following day.

MY DEAR GENERAL: — I went yesterday morning to headquarters, with an intention of speaking to your Excellency, but you were too busy, and I shall state in this letter what I wished to say. I need not tell you how sorry I am at what has lately happened; it is a necessary result of my tender and respectful friendship for you, which is as true and candid as the other sentiments of my heart, and much stronger than so new an acquaintance might seem to admit. But another reason for my concern is my ardent and perhaps enthusiastic wish for the happiness and liberty of this country. I see plainly that America can defend herself, if proper measures are taken; but I begin to fear that she may be lost by herself and her own sons.

"When I was in Europe, I thought that here almost every man was a lover of liberty, and would rather die free than live a slave. You can conceive my astonishment when I saw that Toryism was as apparently professed as Whigism itself. There are open dissensions in Congress; parties who hate one another as much as the common enemy; men who, without knowing anything about war, undertake to judge you, and to make ridiculous comparisons. They are infatuated with Gates, without thinking of the difference of circumstances, and believe that attacking is the only thing necessary to conquer. These ideas are entertained by some jealous men, and perhaps secret friends of the British government, who want to push you, in a moment of ill humor, to some rash enterprise upon the lines, or against a much stronger army.

"I should not take the liberty of mentioning these particulars to you, if I had not received a letter from a young, good-natured gentleman at Yorktown, whom Conway has ruined by his cunning and bad advice, but who entertains the greatest respect for you. I have been surprised to see the poor establishment of the Board of War, the difference made between northern and southern departments, and the orders from Congress about military operations. But the promotion of Conway is beyond all my expectations. I should be glad to have new major-generals, because, as I know that you take some interest in my happiness and reputation, it will perhaps afford an occasion for your Excellency to give me more agreeable commands in some instances. On the other hand, General Conway says he is entirely a man to be disposed of by me, he calls himself my soldier, and the reason of such behavior towards me is, that he wishes to be well spoken of at the French Court; and his protector, the Marquis de Castries, is an intimate acquaintance of mine.

"But since the letter of Lord Stirling, I have inquired into his character, and found that he is an ambitious and dangerous man. He has done all in his power to draw off my confidence and affection from you. His desire was to engage me to leave this country. I now see all the general officers of the army against Congress. Such disputes, if known to the enemy, may be attended with the worst consequences. I am very sorry whenever I perceive troubles raised among defenders of the same cause; but my concern is much greater, when I find officers coming from France, officers of some character in my country, to whom a fault of that kind may be imputed. The reason for my fondness for Conway was his being a very brave and very good officer. However, that talent for manœuvering, which seems so extraordinary to Congress, is not so very difficult a matter for any man of common sense, who applies himself to it. I must render to General Duportail and some other French officers, who have spoken to me, the justice to say, that I found them as I could wish upon this occasion, although it has made a great noise among many in the army. I wish your Excellency could let them know how necessary you are to them, and engage them at the same time to keep peace and reinstate love among themselves, till the moment when these little disputes shall not be attended with such inconveniences. It would be too great a pity, that slavery, dishonor, ruin, and the unhappiness of a whole nation, should issue from trifling differences betwixt a few men.

"You will perhaps find this letter very unimportant; but I was desirous of explaining to you some of my ideas, because it will contribute to my satisfaction to be convinced, that you, my dear General, who have been so indulgent as to permit me to look on you as a friend, should know my sentiments. I have the warmest love for my country, and for all good Frenchmen. Their success fills my heart with joy; but, Sir, besides that Conway is an Irishman, I want countrymen, who in every point do honor to their country. That gentleman had engaged me, by entertaining my imagination with ideas of glory and shining projects, and I must confess this was a too certain way of deceiving me. I wish to join to the few theories about war, which I possess, and to the few dispositions which nature has given me, the experience of thirty campaigns, in the hope that I should be able to be more useful in my present sphere. My desire of deserving your approbation is strong; and, whenever you shall employ me, you can be certain of my trying every exertion in my power to succeed. I am now bound to your fate, and I shall follow it and sustain it, as well by my sword as by all the means in my power. You will pardon my importunity. Youth and friendship perhaps make me too warm, but I feel the greatest concern at recent events. With the most tender and profound respect, I have the honor to be, &c."

MY DEAR MARQUIS:—Your favor of yesterday conveyed to me fresh proof of that friendship and attachment, which I have happily experienced since the first of our acquaintance, and for which I entertain sentiments of the purest affection. It will ever constitute part of my happiness to know that I stand well in your opinion; because I am satisfied that you can have no views to answer by throwing out false colors, and that you possess a mind too exalted to condescend to low arts and intrigues to acquire a reputation. Happy, thrice happy, would it have been for this army, and the cause we are embarked in, if the same generous spirit had pervaded all the actors in it. But one gentleman, whose name you have mentioned, had, I am confident, far different views. His ambition and great desire of being puffed off, as one of the first officers of the age, could only be equalled by the means which he used to obtain them; but, finding that I was determined not to go beyond the line of my duty to indulge him in the first, nor to exceed the strictest rules of propriety to gratify him in the second, he became my inveterate enemy; and he has, I am persuaded, practised every art to do me an injury, even at the expense of reprobating a measure, which did not succeed, that he himself advised to. How far he may have accomplished his ends, I know not; and, except for considerations of a public nature, I care not; for it is well known, that neither ambitious nor lucrative motives led me to accept my present appointments; in the discharge of which, I have endeavored to observe one steady and uniform system of conduct, which I shall invariably pursue, while I have the honor to command, regardless of the tongue of slander or the powers of detraction. The fatal tendency of disunion is so obvious, that I have in earnest terms exhorted such officers as have expressed their dissatisfaction at General Conway's promotion, to be cool and dispassionate in their decision upon the matter; and I have hopes that they will not suffer any hasty determination to injure the service. At the same time, it must be acknowledged that officers' feelings upon these occasions are not to be restrained, although you may control their actions.

"The other observations contained in your letter have too much truth in them; and it is much to be lamented that things are not now as they formerly were; but we must not, in so great a contest, expect to meet with nothing but sunshine. I have no doubt that everything happens for the best, that we shall triumph over all our misfortunes, and in the end be happy; when, my dear Marquis, if you will give me your company in Virginia, we will laugh at our past difficulties and the folly of others; and I will endeavor, by every civility in my power, to show you how much and how sincerely I am your affectionate and obedient servant."

# FRANCE RECOGNIZES AMERICAN INDEPENDENCE

## By Benjamin Franklin

*THIS letter, written by Franklin in 1778, while serving as the American Commissioner in Paris, to Thomas Cushing, the Colonial statesman whom Dr. Samuel Johnson accused of "aiming at an American crown," announces the conclusion of negotiations with the French Government that began with the sending of Silas Deane to Paris in 1775. Before he was superseded by Franklin, Deane acted as the official United States delegate to the French Court, and, besides securing and transmitting supplies, induced many French officers—by lavish promises—to take service in the American army.*

*While in France Franklin was of great aid in founding the American navy, and especially in furthering the operations of John Paul Jones. He negotiated loans to the United States amounting to many millions of francs. In 1782 he signed the preliminary articles of peace, and the next year (September 3,) he was a signer of the Treaty of Paris.*

. . . I RECEIVED your favor by Mr. Austin, with your most agreeable congratulations on the success of the American arms in the Northern Department. In return, give me leave to congratulate you on the success of our negotiations here, in the completion of the two treaties with his most Christian Majesty: the one of amity and commerce, on the plan of that proposed by Congress, with some good additions; the other of alliance for mutual defence, in which the most Christian king agrees to make a common cause with the United States, if England attempts to obstruct the commerce of his subjects with them; and guarantees to the United

States their liberty, sovereignty, and independence, absolute and unlimited, with all the possessions they now have, or may have, at the conclusion of the war; and the States in return guarantee to him his possessions in the West Indies. The great principle in both treaties is a perfect equality and reciprocity; no advantage to be demanded by France, or privileges in commerce, which the States may not grant to any and every other nation.

In short, the king has treated with us generously and magnanimously; taken no advantage of our present difficulties, to exact terms which we would not willingly grant, when established in prosperity and power. I may add that he has acted wisely, in wishing the friendship contracted by these treaties may be durable, which probably might not be if a contrary conduct had taken place.

Several of the American ships, with stores for the Congress, are now about sailing under the convoy of a French squadron. England is in great consternation, and the minister, on the 17th instant, confessing that all his measures had been wrong and that peace was necessary, proposed two bills for quieting America; but they are full of artifice and deceit, and will, I am confident, be treated accordingly by our country.

I think you must have much satisfaction in so valuable a son, whom I wish safe back to you, and am, with great esteem, etc.,

B. FRANKLIN.

P. S.—The treaties were signed by the plenipotentiaries on both sides February 6th, but are still for some reasons kept secret, though soon to be published. It is understood that Spain will soon accede to the same. The treaties are forwarded to Congress by this conveyance.

# A WARNING AGAINST CONCILIATION

## By Patrick Henry

*INSEPARABLE from the American Revolution is the name of Patrick Henry, the Virginia counterpart of Samuel Adams of Massachusetts, Continental congressman, governor and leader of the patriots. Unfortunately there is no text preserved of a single one of his glowing speeches. The extract below, from a letter, dated Williamsburg, June 18, 1778, to a fellow Virginian, Richard Henry Lee, at that time serving as a member of Congress in Philadelphia, shows his spirit; the issue was a plan of conciliation proposed by Great Britain after the French alliance with the United States. Patrick Henry was then Governor of Virginia.*

*As a member of the second Continental Congress, Lee was recognized as one of the really influential leaders of the revolutionary movement, and he became famous through his motion of June 7, 1776, that the colonies should be free and independent States, a motion followed by the Declaration of Independence.*

. . . BOTH your last letters came to hand to-day. I felt for you, on seeing the order in which the balloting placed the delegates in Congress. It is an effect of that rancorous malice, that has so long followed you, through that arduous path of duty which you have invariably travelled, since America resolved to resist her oppressors. Is it any pleasure to you, to remark, that at the same era in which these men figure against you, public spirit seems to have taken its flight from Virginia? It is too much the case; for the quota of our troops is not half made up, and no chance seems to remain for completing it. The Assembly voted three hundred and fifty horse, and two thousand men, to be forth-

with raised, and to join the grand army. Great bounties are offered, but I fear, the only effect will be, to
expose our State to contempt, for I believe no soldiers
will enlist, especially in the infantry.

Can you credit it; no effort was made for supporting, or restoring public credit! I pressed it warmly on
some, but in vain. This is the reason we get no soldiers. We shall issue fifty or sixty thousand dollars
in cash, to equip the cavalry, and their time is to expire at Christmas. I believe they will not be in the
field before that time. Let not Congress rely on Virginia for soldiers. I tell you my opinion, they will not
be got here until a different spirit prevails. I look at
the past condition of America, as at a dreadful preci-
pice, from which we have escaped, by means of the
generous French, to whom I will be everlastingly
bound by the most heartfelt gratitude. But I must
mistake matters, if some of those men who traduce
you, do not prefer the offers of Britain. You will
have a different game to play now with the commissioners. How comes Governor Johnstone there? I
do not see how it comports with his past life. Surely
Congress will never recede from our French friends.
Salvation to America depends upon our holding fast
our attachment to them. I shall date our ruin from
the moment that it is exchanged for anything Great
Britain can say or do. She can never be cordial with
us. Baffled, defeated, disgraced by her colonies, she
will ever meditate revenge.

We can find no safety but in her ruin, or at least in her extreme humiliation, which has not happened, and cannot happen until she is deluged with blood, or thoroughly purged by a revolution, which shall wipe from existence the present King with his connections, and the present system, with those who aid and abet it. For God's sake, my dear sir, quit not the councils of your country, until you see us forever disjoined from Great Britain. The old leaven still works. The flesh pots of Egypt are still savoury to degenerate palates. Again, we are undone if the French alliance is not religiously observed. Excuse my freedom. I know your love to our country, and this is my motive. May heaven give you health and prosperity.

# THE CAPTURE OF VINCENNES

*By George Rogers Clark*

*THE conquest of the great territory north of the Ohio River by General Clark in 1778-9 was one of the most heroic episodes of the Revolutionary period, and one of the most important in its consequences. By reason of it, the Treaty of Paris denominated the Mississippi instead of the Ohio as our western boundary.*

*Clark, whose Memoirs were written at the special request of Jefferson and Madison, and from which this article was taken, was sent by Governor Patrick Henry to subjugate the North-west with a force of less than 200 men. Suffering almost incredible hardships, they placed the country under control of Virginia.*

*Clark died in poverty near Louisville, Ky. Late in life, when his native State sent him a sword, he exclaimed: "When Virginia needed a sword, I gave her one. She now sends me a toy. I want bread!"—thrust the sword in the ground and broke it with his crutch.*

EVERYTHING being ready, on the 5th of February, after receiving a lecture and absolution from the priest, we crossed the Kaskasia River with one hundred and seventy men, marched about three miles and encamped, where we lay until the 7th, and set out. The weather wet (but fortunately not cold for the season) and a great part of the plains under water several inches deep. It was difficult and very fatiguing marching. My object was now to keep the men in spirits. I suffered them to shoot game on all occasions, and feast on it like Indian war-dancers, each company by turns inviting the others to their feasts, which was the case every night, as the company that was to give the feast was always supplied with horses to lay up a sufficient store of wild meat in the course of the day,

myself and principal officers putting on the woodsmen, shouting now and then, and running as much
through the mud and water as any of them. . . .
Crossing a narrow deep lake in the canoes, and
marching some distance, we came to a copse of timber
called the Warrior's Island. We were now in full
view of the fort and town, not a shrub between us,
at about two miles' distance. Every man now feasted
his eyes, and forgot that he had suffered anything,
saying that all that had passed was owing to good
policy and nothing but what a man could bear; and
that a soldier had no right to think, etc.,—passing
from one extreme to another, which is common in
such cases. It was now we had to display our abilities. The plain between us and the town was not a
perfect level. The sunken grounds were covered with
water full of ducks. We observed several men out
on horseback, shooting them, within a half mile of us,
and sent out as many of our active young Frenchmen
to decoy and take one of these men prisoner in such
a manner as not to alarm the others, which they did.
The information we got from this person was similar
to that which we got from those we took on the river,
except that of the British having that evening completed the wall of the fort, and that there was a good
many Indians in town.

Our situation was now truly critical,—no possibility of retreating in case of defeat, and in full view of
a town that had, at this time, upward of six hundred
men in it,—troops, inhabitants and Indians. The

crew of the galley, though not fifty men, would have been now a reënforcement of immense magnitude to our little army (if I may so call it), but we would not think of them. We were now in the situation that I had labored to get ourselves in. The idea of being made prisoner was foreign to almost every man, as they expected nothing but torture from the savages, if they fell into their hands. Our fate was now to be determined, probably in a few hours. We knew that nothing but the most daring conduct would insure success. I knew that a number of the inhabitants wished us well, that many were lukewarm to the interest of either, and I also learned that the grand chief, the Tobacco's son, had but a few days before openly declared, in council with the British, that he was a brother and friend to the Big Knives. These were favorable circumstances; and, as there was but little probability of our remaining until dark undiscovered, I determined to begin the career immediately, and wrote the following placard to the inhabitants:—

To THE INHABITANTS OF VINCENNES:

Gentlemen,—Being now within two miles of your village, with my army, determined to take your fort this night, and not being willing to surprise you, I take this method to request such of you as are true citizens and willing to enjoy the liberty I bring you to remain still in your houses; and those, if any there be, that are friends to the King will instantly repair to the fort, and join the hair-buyer general, and fight like men. And, if any such as do not go to the fort shall be discovered afterward, they may depend on severe punishment. On the contrary, those who are true friends to liberty may depend on being well treated; and I once more request them to keep out of the streets. For every one I find in arms on my arrival I shall treat him as an enemy.

      (Signed)                G. R. CLARK.

. . . We anxiously viewed this messenger until he entered the town, and in a few minutes could discover by our glasses some stir in every street that we could penetrate into, and great numbers running or riding out into the commons, we supposed, to view us, which was the case. But what surprised us was that nothing had yet happened that had the appearance of the garrison being alarmed,—no drum nor gun. We began to suppose that the information we got from our prisoners was false, and that the enemy already knew of us, and were prepared. . . . A little before sunset we moved, and displayed ourselves in full view of the town, crowds gazing at us. . . .

We moved on slowly in full view of the town; but, as it was a point of some consequence to us to make ourselves appear formidable, we, in leaving the covert that we were in, marched and countermarched in such a manner that we appeared numerous. . . .

The firing now commenced on the fort, but they did not believe it was an enemy until one of their men was shot down through a port, as drunken Indians frequently saluted the fort after night. The drums now sounded, and the business fairly commenced on both sides.  Reënforcements were sent to the attack of the garrison, while other arrangements were making in town. . . . We now found that the garrison had known nothing of us; that, having finished the fort that evening, they had amused themselves at different games, and had just retired before my letter arrived, as it was near roll-call.  The placard being made public, many of the inhabitants were afraid to show themselves out of the houses for fear of giving offense, and not one dare give information. . . .

The garrison was soon completely surrounded, and the firing continued without intermission (except about fifteen minutes a little before day) until about nine o'clock the following morning.  It was kept up by the whole of the troops, joined by a few of the young men of the town, who got permission, except fifty men kept as a reserve. . . . I had made myself fully acquainted with the situation of the fort and town and the parts relative to each.  The cannon of the garrison was on the upper floors of strong block-houses at each angle of the fort, eleven feet above the surface, and the ports so badly cut that many of our troops lay under the fire of them within twenty or thirty yards of the walls.  They did no damage, except to the buildings of the town, some of which they much shattered; and their musketry, in the dark, employed against woodsmen covered by houses, palings, ditches, the banks of the river, etc., was but of little avail, and did no injury to us except wounding a man or two.  As we could not afford to lose men, great care

was taken to preserve them sufficiently covered, and
to keep up a hot fire in order to intimidate the enemy
as well as to destroy them. . . . A little before day
the troops were withdrawn from their positions about
the fort, except a few parties of observation, and the
firing totally ceased.  Orders were given, in case of
Lamotte's approach, not to alarm or fire on him without a certainty of killing or taking the whole.  In less
than a quarter of an hour, he passed within ten feet of
an officer and a party that lay concealed.  Ladders
were flung over to them; and, as they mounted them,
our party shouted.  Many of them fell from the top
of the walls,—some within, and others back; but, as
they were not fired on, they all got over, much to the
joy of their friends.  But, on considering the matter,
they must have been convinced that it was a scheme
of ours to let them in, and that we were so strong as to
care but little about them or the manner of their getting into the garrison. . . .

The firing immediately commenced on both sides
with double vigor; and I believe that more noise could
not have been made by the same number of men.
Their shouts could not be heard for the firearms; but
a continual blaze was kept around the garrison, without much being done, until about daybreak, when our
troops were drawn off to posts prepared for them,
about sixty or seventy yards from the fort.  A loop-
hole then could scarcely be darkened but a rifle-ball
would pass through it.  To have stood to their cannon
would have destroyed their men, without a probability

of doing much service.  Our situation was nearly similar.  It would have been imprudent in either party to have wasted their men, without some decisive stroke required it.

Thus the attack continued until about nine o'clock on the morning of the 24th.  Learning that the two prisoners they had brought in the day before had a considerable number of letters with them, I supposed it an express that we expected about this time, which I knew to be of the greatest moment to us, as we had not received one since our arrival in the country; and, not being fully acquainted with the character of our enemy, we were doubtful that those papers might be destroyed, to prevent which I sent a flag [with a letter] demanding the garrison. . . .

We met at the church, about eighty yards from the fort, Lieutenant-governor Hamilton, Major Hay, superintendent of Indian affairs, Captain Helm, their prisoner, Major Bowman, and myself.  The conference began.  Hamilton produced terms of capitulation, signed, that contained various articles, one of which was that the garrison should be surrendered on their being permitted to go to Pensacola on parole. After deliberating on every article, I rejected the whole.  He then wished that I would make some proposition.  I told him that I had no other to make than what I had already made,—that of his surrendering as prisoners at discretion.  I said that his troops had behaved with spirit; that they could not suppose that they would be worse treated in consequence of it;

that, if he chose to comply with the demand, though hard, perhaps the sooner the better; that it was in vain to make any proposition to me; that he, by this time, must be sensible that the garrison would fall; that both of us must [view?] all blood spilt for the future by the garrison as murder; that my troops were already impatient, and called aloud for permission to tear down and storm the fort. . . .

We took our leave, and parted but a few steps, when Hamilton stopped, and politely asked me if I would be so kind as to give him my reasons for refusing the garrison any other terms than those I had offered. I told him I had no objections in giving him my real reasons, which were simply these: that I knew the greater part of the principal Indian partisans of Detroit were with him; that I wanted an excuse to put them to death or otherwise treat them as I thought proper; that the cries of the widows and the fatherless on the frontiers, which they had occasioned, now required their blood from my hand; and that I did not choose to be so timorous as to disobey the absolute commands of their authority, which I looked upon to be next to divine; that I would rather lose fifty men than not to empower myself to execute this piece of business with propriety; that, if he chose to risk the massacre of his garrison for their sakes, it was his own pleasure; and that I might, perhaps, take it into my head to send for some of those widows to see it executed.

Major Hay paying great attention, I had observed a kind of distrust in his countenance, which in a great

measure influenced my conversation during this time.
On my concluding, "Pray, sir," said he, "who is it that
you call Indian partisans?" "Sir," I replied, "I take
Major Hay to be one of the principal." I never saw a
man in the moment of execution so struck as he appeared to be,—pale and trembling, scarcely able to
stand. Hamilton blushed, and, I observed, was much
affected at his behavior. Major Bowman's countenance sufficiently explained his disdain for the one
and his sorrow for the other. . . . Some moments
elapsed without a word passing on either side. From
that moment my resolutions changed respecting Hamilton's situation. I told him that we would return to
our respective posts; that I would reconsider the matter, and let him know the result. No offensive measures should be taken in the meantime. Agreed to;
and we parted. What had passed being made known
to our officers, it was agreed that we should moderate
our resolutions.

In the course of the afternoon of the 24th the following articles were signed:—

I. Lieutenant-governor Hamilton engages to deliver up to Colonel Clark Fort Sackville, as it is at
present, with all the stores, etc.

II. The garrison are to deliver themselves as prisoners of war, and march out with their arms and ac-
couterments, etc.

III. The garrison to be delivered up at ten o'clock
to-morrow.

IV. Three days time to be allowed the garrison to
settle their accounts with the inhabitants and traders
of this place.

V.  The officers of the garrison to be allowed their necessary baggage, etc.

Signed at Post St. Vincent [Vincennes] 24th of February, 1779.

Agreed for the following reasons: the remoteness from succor; the state and quantity of provisions, etc.; unanimity of officers and men in its expediency; the honorable terms allowed; and, lastly, the confidence in a generous enemy.

The business being now nearly at an end, troops were posted in several strong houses around the garrison and patroled during the night to prevent any deception that might be attempted.  The remainder on duty lay on their arms, and for the first time for many days past got some rest. . . . During the siege, I got only one man wounded.  Not being able to lose many, I made them secure themselves well.  Seven were badly wounded in the fort through ports. . . . Almost every man had conceived a favorable opinion of Lieutenant-governor Hamilton,—I believe what affected myself made some impression on the whole; and I was happy to find that he never deviated, while he stayed with us, from that dignity of conduct that became an officer in his situation.  The morning of the 25th approaching, arrangements were made for receiving the garrison [which consisted of seventy-nine men], and about ten o'clock it was delivered in form; and everything was immediately arranged to the best advantage.

# WAYNE SURPRISES AND STORMS STONY POINT

## WASHINGTON TO CONGRESS

*THIS communication, dated from his headquarters at New Windsor, July 21, 1779, from Washington to John Jay, President of Congress, together with the accompanying report of General Anthony Wayne to Washington of his recapture of Stony Point from the British on July 16, 1779, was first published in the Pennsylvania Gazette and General Advertiser twelve days after the event. It followed an earlier report from Wayne to Washington, dated at Stony Point, July 16, 2 A. M., stating briefly, "The fort and garrison with Colonel Johnston are ours. Our officers and men behaved like men who are determined to be free." These reports were published by order of Congress and kindled widespread enthusiasm in the colonies.*

*With 1,200 men Wayne took 543 prisoners, the American loss being 15 killed and 83 wounded. Following the victory the fortifications were dismantled and the place abandoned, the British re-occupying it soon afterwards.*

ON THE 16th instant I had the honor to inform Congress of a successful attack upon the enemy's post at Stony Point, on the preceding night, by Brigadier-General Wayne, and the corps of light infantry under his command. The ulterior operations in which we have been engaged, have hitherto put it out of my power to transmit the particulars of this interesting event. They will now be found in the inclosed report, which I have received from General Wayne. To the encomiums he has deservedly bestowed on the officers and men under his command, it gives me pleasure to add that his own conduct throughout the whole of this arduous enterprise, merits the warmest approbation of Congress.  He improved upon the plan recommended by me, and executed it in a manner that does signal honor to his judgment and to his bravery.  In a critical moment of the assault, he received a flesh wound in the head with a musket ball, but continued leading on his men with unshaken firmness.

I now beg leave, for the private satisfaction of Congress, to explain the motives which induced me to direct the attempt.

It has been the unanimous sentiment to evacuate the captured post at Stony Point, remove the cannon and stores, and destroy the works, which was accomplished on the night of the 18th, one piece of heavy cannon only excepted.  For want of proper tackling within reach to transport the cannon by land, we were obliged to send them to the fort by water.  The movements of the enemy's vessels created some uneasiness on their account, and induced me to keep one of the pieces for their protection, which finally could not be brought off, without risking more for its preservation than it was worth.  We also lost a galley which was ordered down to cover the boats.  She got under way, on her return the afternoon of the 18th.  The enemy began a severe and continued cannonade upon her, from which having received some injury, which disabled her from proceeding, she was run ashore.  Not being able to get her afloat till late in the floodtide, and one or two of the enemy's vessels under favor of the night, having passed above her, she was set on fire and blown up.

It is probable Congress will be pleased to bestow some marks of consideration upon those officers who distinguished themselves upon this occasion. Every officer and man of the corps deserves great credit, but there were particular ones whose situation placed them foremost in danger, and made their conduct most conspicuous. . . . I forgot to mention, that two flags and two standards were taken, the former belonging to the garrison, and the latter to the 17th regiment. These shall be sent to Congress by the first convenient opportunity.

### WAYNE TO WASHINGTON

I HAVE the honor to give you a full and particular relation of the reduction of this point, by the light-infantry under my command.

On the 15th instant at 12 o'clock we took up our line of march from Sandy-beach, distant 14 miles from this place; the roads being exceedingly bad and narrow, and having to pass over high mountains, through deep morasses, and difficult defiles, we were obliged to move in single files the greatest part of the way. At eight o'clock in the evening, the van arrived at Mr. Springsteel's, within one and a half miles of the enemy, and formed into columns as fast as they came up, agreeable to the order of battle annexed; viz. Colonels Febiger's and Meig's regiments, with Major Hull's detachment, formed the right column; Colonel Butler's regiment and Major Murfree's two companies, the left.   The troops remained in this position until several of the principal officers, with myself, had returned from reconnoitering the works. Half after eleven o'clock, being the hour fixed on, the whole moved forward, the van of the right consisted of one hundred and fifty volunteers, properly officered, who advanced with unloaded muskets and fixed bayonets, under the command of Lieutenant Colonel Fleury; these were preceded by twenty picked men, and a vigilant and brave officer, to remove the abatis and other obstructions.   The van of the left consisted of one hundred volunteers, under the command of Major Steward, with unloaded muskets and fixed bayonets, also preceded by a brave and determined officer, with twenty men, for the same purpose as the other.

At 12 o'clock the assault was to begin on the right and left flanks of the enemy's works, while Major Murfree amused them in front; but a deep morass covering their whole front, and at this time overflowed by the tide, together with other obstructions, rendered the approaches more difficult than were at first apprehended, so that it was about twenty minutes after twelve before the assault began, previous to which I placed myself at the head of Febiger's regiment or right column, and gave the troops the most pointed orders not to fire on any account, but place their whole dependence on the bayonet, which order was literally and faithfully obeyed.   Neither the deep morass, the formidable and double rows of abatis, or

the strong works in front and flank, could damp the
ardor of the troops, who in the face of a most tremendous and incessant fire of musketry, and from
cannon loaded with grape-shot, forced their way at
the point of the bayonet, through every obstacle, both
columns meeting in the center of the enemy's works
nearly at the same instant. Too much praise cannot
be given to Lieutenant Colonel Fleury, (who struck
the enemy's standard with his own hand) and to
Major Steward, who commanded the advanced
parties, for their brave and prudent conduct.

Colonels Butler, Meigs, and Febiger conducted
themselves with that coolness, bravery, and perseverance, that will ever insure success. Lieutenant
Colonel Hays was wounded in the thigh, bravely fighting at the head of his battalion. I should take up too
much of your Excellency's time, was I to particularize
every individual who deserves it, for his bravery on
this occasion. I cannot, however, omit Major Lee,
to whom I am indebted for frequent and very useful
intelligence, which contributed much to the success
of the enterprise, and it is with the greatest pleasure
I acknowledge to you, I was supported in the attack
by all the officers and soldiers under my command,
to the utmost of my wishes. The officers and privates of the artillery exerted themselves in turning the
cannon against Verplanck's Point, and forced them
to cut the cables of their shipping, and run down the
river.

I should be wanting in gratitude was I to omit mentioning Captain Fishbourn and Mr. Archer, my two aids-de-camp, who on every occasion showed the greatest intrepidity, and supported me into the works after I received my wound in passing the last abatis.

Inclosed are the returns of the killed and wounded of the light infantry, as also of the enemy, together with the number of prisoners taken, likewise of the ordnance and stores found in the garrison.

I forgot to mention to your Excellency, that previous to my marching, I had drawn General Muhlenberg into my rear, who with three hundred men of his brigade took post on the opposite side of the marsh so as to be in readiness either to support me, or to cover a retreat in case of accident, and I have no doubt of his faithfully and effectually executing either, had there been any occasion for him.

The humanity of our brave soldiery, who scorned to take the lives of a vanquished foe calling for mercy, reflects the highest honor on them, and accounts for the few of the enemy killed on the occasion.

I am not satisfied with the manner in which I have mentioned the conduct of Lieutenants Gibbons and Knox, the two gentlemen who led the advanced parties of twenty men each—their distinguished bravery deserves the highest commendation—the first belongs to the sixth Pennsylvania regiment, and lost 17 men killed and wounded in the attack; the last belongs to the ninth ditto, who was more fortunate in saving his men though not less exposed.

# THE CAPTURE OF THE SERAPIS BY THE BON HOMME RICHARD

### By Commodore John Paul Jones

*THIS report of the naval battle between the Bon Homme Richard, one of four vessels furnished the United States by France, and the British ship Serapis, was sent by John Paul Jones to Benjamin Franklin, then our commissioner in Paris, and by Franklin was forwarded to Congress. It was written October 3, 1779, on board the Serapis, which Jones and his men had boarded before the Bon Homme Richard sank.*

*Jones, who was the first man to hoist the American flag on a man-of-war, had engaged the vastly superior Serapis, convoying 40 British merchantmen, off the coast of Scotland.*

*In an account of the battle by Lieutenant Richard Dale, of the Bon Homme Richard, we are told that at a certain desperate stage of the fight Jones was hailed by Captain Pearson, of the Serapis, who asked, "Has your ship struck?"—to which Jones answered, "I have not yet begun to fight."*

WHEN I had the honor of writing to you on the 11th of August [1779], previous to my departure from the Road of Groaix, I had before me the most flattering prospect of rendering essential service to the common cause of France and America. I had a full confidence in the voluntary inclination and ability of every captain under my command to assist and support me in my duty with cheerful emulation; and I was persuaded that every one of them would pursue glory in preference to interest. . . .

On the morning of the 23d, the brig from Holland not being in sight, we chased a brigantine that appeared laying to windward. About noon we saw and chased a large ship that appeared coming round Flamborough Head from the northward, and at the same time I manned and armed one of the pilot boats to sail in pursuit of the brigantine, which now appeared to be the vessel that I had forced ashore. Soon after this a fleet of 41 sail appeared off Flamborough Head, bearing N.N.E. This induced me to abandon the single ship which had been anchored in Burlington Bay. I also called back the pilot boat, and hoisted a signal for a general chase. When the fleet discovered us bearing down, all the merchant ships crowded sail towards the shore. The two ships of war that protected the fleet at the same time steered from the land, and made the disposition for the battle. In approaching the enemy, I crowded every possible sail, and made the signal for the line of battle, to which the Alliance showed no attention. Earnest as I was for the action, I could not reach the commodore's ship until seven in the evening. Being then within pistol shot, when he hailed the Bon Homme Richard, we answered him by firing a whole broadside.

The battle, being thus begun, was continued with unremitting fury. Every method was practiced on both sides to gain an advantage, and rake each other; and I must confess that the enemy's ship, being much more manageable than the Bon Homme Richard, gained thereby several times an advantageous situation, in spite of my best endeavors to prevent it. As I had to deal with an enemy of greatly superior force,

I was under the necessity of closing with him, to prevent the advantage which he had over me in point
of maneuver.  It was my intention to lay the Bon
Homme Richard athwart the enemy's bow, but, as
that operation required great dexterity in the management of both sails and helm, and some of our braces
being shot away, it did not exactly succeed to my
wishes.  The enemy's bowsprit, however, came over
the Bon Homme Richard's poop by the mizzen mast,
and I made both ships fast together in that situation,
which by the action of the wind on the enemy's sails
forced her stern close to the Bon Homme Richard's
bow, so that the ships lay square alongside of each
other, the yards being all entangled, and the cannon
of each ship touching the opponent's side.

When this position took place, it was 8 o'clock,
previous to which the Bon Homme Richard had received sundry eighteen-pounds shot below the water,
and leaked very much.  My battery of 12-pounders,
on which I had placed my chief dependence, being
commanded by Lieutenant Dale and Colonel Weibert,
and manned principally with American seamen and
French volunteers, were entirely silenced and abandoned.  As to the six old eighteen-pounders that
formed the battery of the lower gun-deck, they did
no service whatever.  Two out of three of them burst
at the first fire, and killed almost all the men who
were stationed to manage them.  Before this time,
too, Colonel de Chamillard, who commanded a party
of 20 soldiers on the poop, had abandoned that sta-

tion after having lost some of his men. These men deserted their quarters.

I had now only two pieces of cannon, nine-pounders, on the quarter deck, that were not silenced; and not one of the heavier cannon was fired during the rest of the action. The purser, Mr. Mease, who commanded the guns on the quarter deck, being dangerously wounded in the head, I was obliged to fill his place, and with great difficulty rallied a few men, and shifted over one of the lee quarter-deck guns, so that we afterward played three pieces of 9-pounders upon the enemy. The tops alone seconded the fire of this little battery, and held out bravely during the whole of the action, especially the main top, where Lieutenant Stack commanded. I directed the fire of one of the three cannon against the main-mast, with double-headed shot, while the other two were exceedingly well served with grape and canister shot to silence the enemy's musketry, and clear her decks, which was at last effected.

The enemy were, as I have since understood, on the instant of calling for quarters when the cowardice or treachery of three of my under officers induced them to call to the enemy. The English commodore asked me if I demanded quarters; and, I having answered him in the most determined negative, they renewed the battle with double fury. They were unable to stand the deck; but the fire of their cannon, especially the lower battery, which was entirely formed of 18-pounders, was incessant. Both ships were set on fire in various places, and the scene was dreadful beyond the reach of language. To account for the timidity of my three under officers,—I mean the gunner, the carpenter, and the master-at-arms,— I must observe that the two first were slightly wounded; and, as the ship had received various shots under water, and one of the pumps being shot away, the carpenter expressed his fear that she would sink, and the other two concluded that she was sinking, which occasioned the gunner to run aft on the poop without my knowledge to strike the colors. Fortunately for me, a cannon ball had done that before by carrying away the ensign staff. He was therefore reduced to the necessity of sinking, as he supposed, or of calling for quarter; and he preferred the latter.

All this time the Bon Homme Richard had sustained the action alone, and the enemy, though much superior in force, would have been very glad to have got clear, as appears by their own acknowledgments, and by their having let go an anchor the instant that I laid them on board, by which means they would have escaped, had I not made them well fast to the Bon Homme Richard.

At last, at half-past 9 o'clock, the Alliance appeared, and I now thought the battle at an end; but, to my utter astonishment, he discharged a broadside full into the stern of the Bon Homme Richard. We called to him for God's sake to forbear firing into the Bon Homme Richard; yet he passed along the off side of the ship, and continued firing. There was no possibility of his mistaking the enemy's ship for the Bon Homme Richard, there being the most essential difference in their appearance and construction; besides, it was then full moonlight, and the side of the Bon Homme Richard were all black, while the sides of the prizes were yellow; yet, for the greater security, I showed the signal of our reconnoissance by putting out three lanterns, one at the head (bow), another at the stern, (quarter), and the third in the middle in a horizontal line.

Every tongue cried that he was firing into the wrong ship, but nothing availed. He passed round, firing into the Bon Homme Richard's head, stern, and broadside; and by one of his volleys killed several of my best men, and mortally wounded a good officer on the forecastle.

My situation was really deplorable. The Bon Homme Richard received various shot under water from the Alliance, the leak gained on the pumps, and the fire increased much on board both ships. Some officers persuaded me to strike, of whose courage and good sense I entertain a high opinion. My treacherous master-at-arms let loose all my prisoners without my knowledge, and my prospect became gloomy indeed. I would not, however, give up the point. The enemy's main-mast began to shake, their firing decreased, ours rather increased, and the British colors were struck at half an hour past 10 o'clock.

This prize proved to be the British ship of war the Serapis, a new ship of 44 guns, built on their most approved construction, with two complete batteries, one of them of 18-pounders, and commanded by the brave Commodore Richard Pearson. I had yet two enemies to encounter far more formidable than the Britons,—I mean fire and water. The Serapis was attacked only by the first, but the Bon Homme Richard was assailed by both. There were five feet of water in the hold, and, though it was moderate from the explosion of so much gunpowder, the three pumps that remained could with difficulty only keep the water from gaining. Fire broke out in various parts of the ship, in spite of all the water that could be thrown to quench it, and at length broke out as low as the powder magazine, and within a few inches of the powder.

In that dilemma I took out the powder upon deck, ready to be thrown overboard at the last extremity; and it was ten o'clock the next day, the 24th, before the fire was entirely extinguished. With respect to the situation of the Bon Homme Richard, the rudder was cut entirely off the stern frame, and the transoms were almost entirely cut away; the timbers, by the lower deck especially, from the main-mast to the stern, being greatly decayed with age, were mangled beyond my power of description; and a person must have been an eye-witness to form a just idea of the tremendous scene of carnage, wreck, and ruin that everywhere appeared. Humanity cannot but recoil from the prospect of such finished horror, and lament that war should produce such fatal consequences.

After the carpenters, as well as Captain de Cotti-
neau, and other men of sense, had well examined and
surveyed the ship (which was not finished before five
in the evening), I found every person to be convinced
that it was impossible to keep the Bon Homme Richard afloat so as to reach a port if the wind should increase, it being then only a very moderate breeze.
I had but little time to remove my wounded, which
now became unavoidable, and which was effected in
the course of the night and next morning. I was determined to keep the Bon Homme Richard afloat,
and, if possible, to bring her into port. For that purpose the first lieutenant of the Pallas continued on
board with a party of men to attend the pumps, with
boats in waiting ready to take them on board in case
the water should gain on them too fast. The wind
augmented in the night and the next day, on the 25th,
so that it was impossible to prevent the good old ship
from sinking. They did not abandon her till after
9 o'clock. The water was then up to the lower deck,
and a little after ten I saw with inexpressible grief
the last glimpse of the Bon Homme Richard. No
lives were lost with the ship, but it was impossible
to save the stores of any sort whatever. I lost even
the best part of my clothes, books, and papers; and
several of my officers lost all their clothes and
effects. . . .

We this day anchored here [off the Texel, Hol-
land], having since the action been tossed to and fro
by contrary winds. I wished to have gained the Road

of Dunkirk on account of our prisoners, but was overruled by the majority of my colleagues.   I shall hasten
up to Amsterdam; and there, if I meet with no orders
for my government, I will take the advice of the
French ambassador.   It is my present intention to
have the Countess of Scarborough ready to transport
the prisoners from hence to Dunkirk, unless it should
be found more expedient to deliver them to the English ambassador, taking his obligation to send to Dunkirk, &c., immediately an equal number of American
prisoners.   I am under strong apprehensions that our
object here will fail, and that through the imprudence
of M. de Chaumont, who has communicated everything he knew or thought on the matter to persons
who cannot help talking of it at a full table.   This is
the way he keeps state secrets, though he never mentioned the affair to me.

# ARNOLD'S TREASON

*GOADED by what he re-garded as the injustice of Congress in ordering Washington to publicly rebuke him for having abused his military authority and for favoring Tories, although a court-martial had acquitted him of intentional wrong-doing, Benedict Arnold, one of the bravest and most capable officers in the American army, conspired to surrender the important fortress of West Point to the British. On September 23, 1780, three days before Washington wrote the first of the accompanying documents to Colonel Nathaniel Wade, the plot was frustrated by the capture of the British go-between, Major André. On the following day Washington sent the second communication, from his Headquarters at the Robinson house, across the Hudson from West Point, to Congress.*

*"The gentlemen of Arnold's [staff] family" were Colonels Varick and Franck, who, with the Joshua Smith mentioned by Washington, were acquitted of conspiring with Arnold.*

GENERAL ARNOLD is gone to the enemy. I have just received a line from him, inclosing one to Mrs. Arnold, dated on board the Vulture. From this circumstance, and Colonel Lamb's being detached on some business, the command of the garrison for the present devolves upon you. I request you will be as vigilant as possible, and as the enemy may have it in contemplation to attempt some enterprise, e v e n to-night, against these posts, I wish you to make, immediately after receipt of this, the best disposition you can of your force, so as to have a proportion of men in each work on the west side of the river. You will see or hear from me further to-morrow.

I HAVE the honor to inform Congress that I arrived
here [his headquarters in the New York High-
lands] at about twelve o'clock on my return from
Hartford. Some hours previous to my arrival General Arnold went from his quarters, which were this
place, and, as it was supposed, over the river to the
garrison at West Point, whither I proceeded myself,
in order to visit the post.

I found General Arnold had not been there during
the day, and on my return to his quarters he was still
absent. In the meantime a packet had arrived from
Lieutenant Colonel Jameson, announcing the capture
of a John Anderson who was endeavoring to go to
New York with several interesting and important
papers, all in the handwriting of General Arnold.
This was also accompanied with a letter from the
prisoner, avowing himself to be Major John André,
Adjutant to the British army, relating the manner
of his capture, and endeavoring to show that he did
not come under the description of a spy. From these
several circumstances, and information that the general seemed to be thrown into some degree of agita-
tion, on receiving a letter a little time before he went
from his quarters, I was led to conclude immediately
that he had heard of Major André's captivity, and that
he would, if possible, escape to the enemy, and accordingly took such measures as appeared the most
probable to apprehend him. But he had embarked
in a barge and proceeded down the river, under a flag,

to the Vulture ship of war, which lay at some miles below Stony and Verplank's Points.

He wrote me a letter after he got on board. Major André is not arrived yet, but I hope he is secure, and that he will be here to-day.

I have been and am taking precaution which I trust will prove effectual, to prevent the important consequences which this conduct on the part of General Arnold was intended to produce. I do not know the party that took Major André, but it is said that it consisted of only a few militia, who acted in such a manner upon the occasion, as does them the highest honor, and proves them to be men of great virtue. As soon as I know their names, I shall take pleasure in transmitting them to Congress. I have taken such measures with respect to the gentlemen of General Arnold's family, as prudence dictated; but from everything that has hitherto come to my knowledge, I have the greatest reason to believe they are perfectly innocent. I early secured Joshua H. Smith, the person mentioned in the close of General Arnold's letter, and find him to have had considerable share in this business.

### GENERAL NATHANIEL GREENE'S ADDRESS TO THE ARMY

TREASON of the blackest dye was yesterday discovered. General Arnold, who commanded at West Point, lost to every sense of honor, of private and public obligation, was about to deliver up that important post into the hands of the enemy. Such an event must have given the American cause a dangerous, if not a fatal wound; but the treason has been timely discovered, to prevent the fatal misfortune. The providential train of circumstances which led to it affords the most convincing proof that the liberties of America are the object of Divine protection. At the same time that the treason is to be regretted, the general cannot help congratulating the army on the happy discovery.

Our enemies, despairing of carrying their point by force, are practicing every base art to effect by bribery and corruption what they cannot accomplish in a manly way. Great honor is due to the American army that this is the first instance of treason of the kind, where many were to be expected from the nature of the dispute. The brightest ornament in the character of the American soldiers is their having been proof against all the arts and seductions of an insidious enemy. Arnold has made his escape to the enemy, but Major André, the Adjutant General in the British army, who came out as a spy, is our prisoner.

His Excellency the Commander-in-Chief, has arrived at West Point from Hartford, and is no doubt taking proper measures to unravel fully so hellish a plot.

# ANDRÉ, FACING EXECUTION, WRITES TO WASHINGTON

*THE André episode is one of the most painful in Revolutionary history. Major John André, a British officer of high character and standing, representing the British General, Sir Henry Clinton, met General Benedict Arnold, in secret, to arrange the betrayal of West Point, with its stores and magazines, including nearly the whole stock of powder of the American army. After the meeting near West Point André was on his way down the Hudson to New York when captured at Tarrytown. Incriminating documents found on his person brought about his trial, conviction and military execution as a spy, on October 2, 1780.*

*The first of these letters was written by Major André to General Washington on September 24th, the day after his capture. As an appendix to the letter is a paper drawn up by André recounting the facts of the case. The concluding letter was written by André to Washington on the eve of his execution.*

WHAT I have as yet said concerning myself was in the justifiable attempt to be extricated; I am too little accustomed to duplicity to have succeeded.

I beg your Excellency will be persuaded that no alteration in the temper of my mind, or apprehension for my safety, induces me to take the step of addressing you, but that it is to rescue myself from an imputation of having assumed a mean character for treacherous purposes or self-interest; a conduct incompatible with the principles that actuate me, as well as with my condition in life.

It is to vindicate my fame that I speak, and not to solicit security.

The person in your possession is Major John André, adjutant-general to the British army.

286

The influence of one commander in the army of his adversary is an advantage taken in war. A correspondence for this purpose I held; as confidential (in the present instance) with his Excellency Sir Henry Clinton.

To favor it, I agreed to meet upon ground not within the posts of either army, a person who was to give me intelligence; I came up in the Vulture man-of-war for this effect, and was fetched by a boat from the ship to the beach. Being there, I was told that the approach of day would prevent my return, and that I must be concealed until the next night. I was in my regimentals and had fairly risked my person.

Against my stipulation, my intention, and without my knowledge beforehand, I was conducted within one of your posts. Your Excellency may conceive my sensation on this occasion, and will imagine how much more must I have been affected by a refusal to reconduct me back the next night as I had been brought. Thus become a prisoner, I had to concert my escape. I quitted my uniform, and was passed another way in the night, without the American posts, to neutral ground, and informed I was beyond all armed parties and left to press for New York. I was taken at Tarrytown by some volunteers.

Thus, as I have had the honor to relate, was I betrayed (being adjutant-general of the British army) into the vile condition of an enemy in disguise within your posts.

Having avowed myself a British officer, I have nothing to reveal but what relates to myself, which is true on the honor of an officer and a gentleman.

The request I have to make to your Excellency, and I am conscious I address myself well, is, that in any rigor policy may dictate, a decency of conduct towards me may mark, that though unfortunate I am branded with nothing dishonorable, as no motive could be mine but the service of my King, and as I was involuntarily an impostor.

Another request is, that I may be permitted to write an open letter to Sir Henry Clinton, and another to a friend for clothes and linen.

I take the liberty to mention the condition of some gentlemen at Charleston, who, being either on parole or under protection, were engaged in a conspiracy against us. Though their situation is not similar, they are objects who may be set in exchange for me, or are persons whom the treatment I receive might affect.

It is no less, Sir, in a confidence of the generosity of your mind, than on account of your superior station, that I have chosen to importune you with this letter. I have the honor to be, with great respect, Sir, your Excellency's most obedient humble servant.

\*　　\*　　\*　　\*　　\*

ON the 20th of September, I left New York to get on board the Vulture, in order (as I thought) to meet General Arnold there in the night. No boat, however, came off, and I waited on board until the night of the 21st. During the day, a flag of truce was

sent from the Vulture to complain of the violation
of a military rule in the instance of a boat having been
decoyed on shore by a flag, and fired upon.   The letter was addressed to General Arnold, signed by Captain Sutherland, but written in my hand and counter-
signed "J. Anderson, secretary."   Its intent was to
indicate my presence on board the Vulture.   In the
night of the 21st a boat with Mr. Smith and two
hands came on board, in order to fetch Mr. Anderson
on shore, and, if too late to bring me back, to lodge
me until the next night in a place of safety.   I went
into the boat, landed, and spoke with Arnold.   I got
on horseback with him to proceed to Smith's house,
and in the way passed a guard I did not expect to see,
having Sir Henry Clinton's directions not to go within
an enemy's post, or to quit my own dress.

In the morning A. quitted me, having himself made
me put the papers I bore between my stockings and
feet.   Whilst he did it, he expressed a wish in case
of any accident befalling me, that they should be destroyed, which I said, of course would be the case,
as when I went into the boat I should have them tied
about with a string and a stone.   Before we parted,
some mention had been made of my crossing the
river, and going by another route; but, I objected
much against it, and thought it was settled that in the
way I came I was also to return.

Mr. Smith to my great mortification persisted in his
determination of carrying me by the other route; and,
at the decline of the sun, I set out on horseback,
passed King's Ferry, and came to Crompond, where a

party of militia stopped us and advised we should remain. In the morning I came with Smith as far as within two miles and a half of Pine's Bridge, where he said he must part with me, as the Cow-boys infested the road thenceforward. I was now near thirty miles from Kingsbridge, and left to the chance of passing that space undiscovered. I got to the neighborhood of Tarrytown, which was far beyond the points described as dangerous, when I was taken by three volunteers, who, not satisfied with my pass, rifled me, and, finding papers, made me a prisoner.

I have omitted mentioning, that, when I found myself within an enemy's posts, I changed my dress.

＊　　＊　　＊　　＊　　＊

BUOYED above the terror of death, by the consciousness of a life devoted to honorable pursuits, and stained with no action that can give me remorse, I trust that the request I make to your Excellency at this serious period, and which is to soften my last moments, will not be rejected.

Sympathy towards a soldier will surely induce your Excellency and a military tribunal to adapt the mode of my death to the feelings of a man of honor.

Let me hope, Sir, that if aught in my character impresses you with esteem towards me, if aught in my misfortunes marks me as the victim of policy and not of resentment, I shall experience the operation of these feelings in your breast, by being informed that I am not to die on a gibbet.

I have the honor to be your Excellency's most obedient and most humble servant.

# THE EXECUTION OF ANDRÉ

*By General William Heath*

*GENERAL HEATH, a witness of the hanging of André, had been assigned to the command of the Hudson River posts in 1779, and except for a short interval remained there until the close of the war. His memoirs, from which this account, dated October 2, 1780, was taken, were published in 1798 by authority of Congress.*

*The hanging of André took place at Tappan, a hamlet in Rockland County, south of Nyack, N. Y. A monument, erected there by Cyrus W. Field, has several times been partly destroyed and then restored. A tablet to André's memory was placed in Westminster Abbey early in the nineteenth century, and in 1821 his body was disinterred at Tappan and conveyed to Westminster Abbey.*

MAJOR ANDRÉ is no more among the living. I have just witnessed his exit. It was a tragical scene of the deepest interest. During his confinement and trial, he exhibited those proud and elevated sensibilities which designate greatness and dignity of mind. Not a murmur or a sigh ever escaped him, and the civilities and attentions bestowed on him were politely acknowledged.

Having left a mother and two sisters in England, he was heard to mention them in terms of the tenderest affection, and in his letter to Sir Henry Clinton, he recommends them to his particular attention.

The principal guard officer who was constantly in the room with the prisoner, relates that when the hour of his execution was announced to him in the morning, he received it without emotion, and while all present were affected with silent gloom, he retained a firm countenance, with calmness and composure of mind. Observing his servant enter the room in tears, he exclaimed, "Leave me till you can show yourself more manly."

His breakfast being sent to him from the table of General Washington, which had been done every day of his confinement, he partook of it as usual, and having shaved and dressed himself, he placed his hat on the table, and cheerfully said to the guard officers, "I am ready at any moment, gentlemen, to wait on you."

The fatal hour having arrived, a large detachment of troops was paraded, and an immense concourse of people assembled; almost all our general and field officers, excepting his Excellency and his staff, were present on horseback; melancholy and gloom pervaded all ranks, and the scene was affectingly awful. I was so near during the solemn march to the fatal spot, as to observe every movement, and share in every emotion which the sad scene was calculated to produce.

Major André walked from the stone house, in which he had been confined, between two of our subaltern officers, arm in arm; the eyes of the immense multitude were fixed on him, who, rising superior to the fears of death, appeared as if conscious of the dignity which he displayed.

He betrayed no want of fortitude, but retained a complacent smile on his countenance, and politely bowed to several gentlemen whom he knew, which was respectfully returned. It was his earnest desire to be shot, as being the mode of death most fitting to the feelings of a military man, and he had indulged the hope that his request would be granted.

At the moment, therefore, when suddenly he came in view of the gallows, he involuntarily started backwards, and made a pause. "Why this emotion, sir?" said an officer by his side. Instantly recovering his composure, he said, "I am reconciled to my death, but I detest the mode." While waiting and standing near the gallows, I observed some degree of trepidation; placing his foot on a stone, and rolling it over and choking in his throat, as if attempting to swallow.

So soon, however, as he perceived that things were in readiness, he stepped quickly into the wagon, and at this moment he appeared to shrink, but instantly elevating his head with firmness, he said, "It will be but a momentary pang," and he took from his pocket two white handkerchiefs; the provost marshal with one loosely pinioned his arms, and with the other, the victim, after taking off his hat and stock, bandaged his own eyes with perfect firmness, which melted the hearts, and moistened the cheeks, not only of his servant, but of the throng of spectators.

When the rope was appended to the gallows, he slipped the noose over his head and adjusted it to his neck, without the assistance of the awkward executioner. Colonel Scammel now informed him that he had an opportunity to speak, if he desired it; he raised the handkerchief from his eyes and said, "I pray you to bear me witness that I meet my fate like a brave man."

The wagon being now removed from under him, he was suspended and instantly expired; it proved indeed "but a momentary pang." He was dressed in his royal regimentals and boots, and his remains, in the same dress, were placed in an ordinary coffin, and interred at the foot of the gallows; and the spot was consecrated by the tears of thousands. Thus died in the bloom of life, the accomplished Major André, the pride of the royal army.

# THE LAST DAYS OF THE REVOLUTION

## By James Madison

*MADISON was at this time (1780-81) a young Virginia lawyer who had graduated, nine years earlier, from Princeton College. Already he had been a delegate, in 1776, to the Revolutionary convention of Virginia and was a member of the first Legislature elected under the Virginia Constitution.*

*This review of the final events and battles of the war, which was rapidly approaching its end at Yorktown, was written while Madison was a member of the Continental Congress sitting in Philadelphia. Later he coöperated with Alexander Hamilton and John Jay in producing the famous publication known as the Federalist, which powerfully influenced popular opinion in favor of the Constitution. About thirty of the eighty odd papers of that work are attributed to him.*

THE insuperable difficulties which opposed a general conquest of America seemed as early as the year 1779 to have been felt by the enemy, and to have led them into the scheme of directing their operations and views against the Southern States only. Clinton accordingly removed with the principal part of his force from New York to South Carolina, and laid siege to Charleston, which, after an honorable resistance, was compelled to surrender to a superiority of force. Our loss in men, besides the inhabitants of the town, was not less than two thousand. Clinton returned to New York. Cornwallis was left with about five thousand troops to pursue his conquests. General Gates was appointed to the command of the Southern department, in place of Lincoln, who commanded in Charleston at the time of its capitulation. He met Cornwallis on the

16th of August, 1780, near Camden, in the upper part of South Carolina and on the border of North Carolina. A general action ensued, in which the American troops were defeated with considerable loss, though not without making the enemy pay a good price for their victory. Cornwallis continued his progress into North Carolina, but afterwards retreated to Camden.

The defeat of Gates was followed by so general a clamor against him, that it was judged expedient to recall him. Greene was sent to succeed in the command. About the time of his arrival at the army, Cornwallis, having been reinforced from New York, resumed his enterprise into North Carolina. A detachment of his best troops was totally defeated by Morgan with an inferior number, and consisting of a major part of militia detached from Greene's army. Five hundred were made prisoners, between two and three hundred killed and wounded, and about the like number escaped. This disaster, instead of checking the ardor of Cornwallis, afforded a new incentive to a rapid advance, in the hope of recovering his prisoners. The vigilance and activity, however, of Morgan, secured them. Cornwallis continued his pursuit as far as the Dan river, which divides North Carolina from Virginia. Greene, whose inferior force obliged him to recede this far before the enemy, received such succors of militia on his entering Virginia that the chase was reversed. Cornwallis, in his turn, retreated precipitately. Greene overtook him on his way to Wilmington, and attacked him. Although the ground

was lost on our side, the British army was so much
weakened by the loss of five or six hundred of their
best troops, that their retreat towards Wilmington
suffered little interruption.

Greene pursued as long as any chance of reaching
his prey remained, and then, leaving Cornwallis on
his left, took an oblique direction towards Camden,
which, with all the other posts in South Carolina except Charleston and Ninety-Six, have, in consequence,
fallen again into our possession. His army lay before
the latter when we last heard from him. It contained
seven or eight hundred men and large quantities of
stores. It is nearly two hundred miles from Charleston, and, without some untoward accident, cannot
fail of being taken. Greene has detachments all over
South Carolina, some of them within a little distance
of Charleston; and the resentments of the people
against their late insolent masters ensure him all the
aids they can give in reëstablishing the American
Government there. Great progress is also making in
the redemption of Georgia.

As soon as Cornwallis had refreshed his troops at
Wilmington, abandoning his Southern conquests to
their fate, he pushed forward into Virginia. The
parricide Arnold had a detachment at Portsmouth
when he lay on the Dan; Philips had reinforced him
so powerfully from New York, that the junction of
the two armies at Petersburg could not be prevented.
The whole force amounted to about six thousand
men. The force under the Marquis de Lafayette,
who commanded in Virginia, being greatly inferior,

did not oppose them, but retreated into Orange and Culpeper in order to meet General Wayne, who was on his way from Pennsylvania to join him. Cornwallis advanced northward as far as Chesterfield, in the county of Caroline, having parties at the same time at Page's warehouse and other places in its vicinity. A party of horse, commanded by Tarleton, was sent with all the secrecy and celerity possible to surprise and take the General Assembly and Executive who had retreated from Richmond to Charlottesville. The vigilance of a young gentleman who discovered the design and rode express to Charlottesville prevented a complete surprise. As it was, several delegates were caught, and the rest were within an hour of sharing the same fate. Among the captives was Colonel Lyon of Hanover. Mr. Kinlock, a member of Congress from South Carolina, was also caught at Mr. John Walker's, whose daughter he had married some time before. Governor Jefferson had a very narrow escape. The members of the Government rendezvoused at Stanton, where they soon made a House.

Mr. Jefferson's year having expired, he declined a reëlection, and General Nelson has taken his place. Tarleton's party retreated with as much celerity as it had advanced. On the junction of Wayne with the Marquis and the arrival of militia, the latter faced about and advanced rapidly on Cornwallis, who retreated to Richmond, and thence precipitately to Williamsburg, where he lay on the 27th ultimo. The Marquis pursued, and was at the same time within twenty miles of that place. One of his advanced parties had had a successful skirmish within six miles of Williamsburg. Bellini has, I understand, abided patiently in the college the dangers and inconveniences of such a situation. I do not hear that the consequences have condemned the experiment. Such is the present state of the war in the Southern Department.

In the Northern, the operations have been for a considerable time in a manner suspended. At present, a vigorous siege of New York by General Washington's army, aided by five or six thousand French troops under Count de Rochambeau, is in contemplation, and will soon commence. As the English have the command of the water, the result of such an enterprise must be very uncertain. It is supposed, however, that it will certainly oblige the enemy to withdraw their force from the Southern States, which may be a more convenient mode of relieving them than by marching the troops from New York at this season of the year to the southward. On the whole, the probable conclusion of this campaign is, at this juncture, very flattering, the enemy being on the defensive in every quarter. . . .

The great advantage the enemy have over us lies in the superiority of their navy, which enables them continually to shift the war into defenseless places, and to weary out our troops by long marches. The squadron sent by our ally to our support did not arrive till a reinforcement on the part of the enemy had counteracted their views. They have been almost constantly blocked up at Rhode Island by the British fleet. The effects of a hurricane in the last spring on the latter gave a temporary advantage to the former, but circumstances delayed the improvement of it till the critical season was past. Mr. Destouches, who commanded the French fleet, nevertheless hazarded an expedition into Chesapeake Bay. The object of it was to coöperate with the Marquis de Lafayette in an attack against Arnold, who lay at Portsmouth with about fifteen hundred British troops. Had he got into the bay, and taken a favorable station, the event would certainly have been adequate to our hopes. Unfortunately, the British fleet, which followed the French immediately from Rhode Island, reached the capes of Virginia first. On the arrival of the latter, a regular and fair combat took place. It lasted for several hours, and ended rather in favor of our allies. As the enemy, however, were nearest the capes, and one of the French ships had lost her rudder, and was otherwise much damaged, the commander thought it best to relinquish his object, and return to his former station. The damage sustained by the enemy, according to their own representation, exceeded that of the French; and as their number of ships and weight of metal were both superior, it does great honor to the gallantry and good conduct of Mr. Destouches. Congress, and indeed the public at large, were so sensible of this, that their particular thanks were given him on the occasion.

# THE BATTLE OF YORKTOWN

## By General Charles Cornwallis

*OUT of the many journals and letters written by participants in the Virginia campaign, this account of the battle and capitulation of Yorktown, addressed by Cornwallis to the British Commander-in-Chief in America, Sir Henry Clinton, is given as the official statement of the defeated general. It was dated from Yorktown, October 20, 1781.*

*Cornwallis had served under Clinton at the reduction of Charleston, S. C., the year before, and subsequently had defeated Gates at Camden, S. C., and Greene at Guilford Court House, N. C., before sweeping against Lafayette in Virginia. The trap laid by Lafayette in conjunction with Washington and Rochambeau on land, aided by a French fleet under De Grasse, was sprung, and Cornwallis, to escape annihilation, surrendered on October 19—virtually ending the Revolutionary War.*

I HAVE the mortification to inform your Excellency that I have been forced to give up the Posts of York and Gloucester, and to surrender the troops under my command, by capitulation, on the 19th instant, as prisoners of war to the combined forces of America and France.

I never saw this post in a very favorable light, but when I found I was to be attacked in it in so unprepared a state, by so powerful an army and artillery, nothing but the hopes of relief would have induced me to attempt its defense, for I would either have endeavored to escape to New York by rapid marches from the Gloucester side, immediately on the arrival of General Washington's troops at Williamsburg, or I would, notwithstanding the disparity of numbers, have at-

tacked them in the open field, where it might have
been just possible that fortune would have favored
the gallantry of the handful of troops under my command, but being assured by your Excellency's letters
that every possible means would be tried by the navy
and army to relieve us, I could not think myself at
liberty to venture upon either of those desperate attempts; therefore, after remaining for two days in a
strong position in front of this place in hopes of being
attacked, upon observing that the enemy were taking
measures which could not fail of turning my left flank
in a short time, and receiving on the second evening
your letter of the 24th of September, informing me
that the relief would sail about the 5th of October, I
withdrew within the works on the night of the 29th
of September, hoping by the labor and firmness of
the soldiers to protract the defense until you could
arrive.  Everything was to be expected from the spirit
of the troops, but every disadvantage attended their
labor, as the works were to be continued under the
enemy's fire, and our stock of intrenching tools, which
did not much exceed 400 when we began to work in
the latter end of August, was now much diminished.

The enemy broke ground on the night of the 30th,
and constructed on that night, and the two following
days and nights, two redoubts, which, with some
works that had belonged to our outward position, occupied a gorge between two creeks or ravines, which
come from the river on each side of the town.  On
the night of the 6th of October they made their first

parallel, extending from its right on the river, to a deep ravine on the left, nearly opposite to the center of this place, and embracing our whole left at a distance of 600 yards. Having perfected this parallel, their batteries opened on the evening of the 9th against our left, and other batteries fired at the same time against a redoubt advanced over the creek upon our right, and defended by about 120 men of the 23rd regiment and marines, who maintained that post with uncommon gallantry. The fire continued incessant from heavy cannon, and from mortars and howitzers throwing shells from 8 to 16 inches, until all our guns on the left were silenced, our work much damaged, and our loss of men considerable. On the night of the 11th they began their second parallel, about 300 yards nearer to us. The troops being much weakened by sickness, as well as by the fire of the besiegers, and observing that the enemy had not only secured their flanks, but proceeded in every respect with the utmost regularity and caution, I could not venture so large sorties as to hope from them any considerable effect, but otherwise, I did everything in my power to interrupt this work by opening new embrasures for guns and keeping up a constant fire from all the howitzers and small mortars that we could man.

On the evening of the 14th they assaulted and carried two redoubts that had been advanced about 300 yards for the purpose of delaying their approaches, and covering our left flank, and during the night included them in their second parallel, on which they continued to work with the utmost exertion. Being perfectly sensible that our works could not stand many hours after the opening of the batteries of that parallel, we not only continued a constant fire with all our mortars and every gun that could be brought to bear upon it, but a little before daybreak on the morning of the 16th, I ordered a sortie of about 350 men, under the direction of Lieut.-Colonel Abercrombie, to attack two batteries which appeared to be in the greatest forwardness, and to spike the guns. A detachment of Guards with the 80th company of Grenadiers, under the command of Lieut.-Colonel Lake, attacked the one, and one of light infantry, under the command of Major Armstrong, attacked the other, and both succeeded in forcing the redoubts that covered them, spiking 11 guns, and killing or wounding about 100 of the French troops, who had the guard of that part of the trenches, and with little loss on our side.

This action, though extremely honorable to the officers and soldiers who executed it, proved of little public advantage, for the cannon having been spiked in a hurry, were soon rendered fit for service again, and before dark the whole parallel and batteries appeared to be nearly complete. At this time we knew that there was no part of the whole front attacked on which we could show a single gun, and our shells were nearly expended. I, therefore, had only to choose between preparing to surrender next day, or endeavor-

The Moore House at Yorktown, Virginia, Where Washington Met and Read to Cornwallis the Terms of Surrender

ing to get off with the greatest part of the troops, and
I determined to attempt the latter. . . .

In this situation, with my little force divided, the
enemy's batteries opened at daybreak.  The passage
between this place and Gloucester was much exposed,
but the boats having now returned, they were ordered
to bring back the troops that had passed during the
night, and they joined us in the forenoon without
much loss.  Our works, in the meantime, were going
to ruin, and not having been able to strengthen them
by an abattis, nor in any other manner but by a slight
fraizing, which the enemy's artillery were demolish-
ing wherever they fired, my opinion entirely coincided
with that of the engineer and principal officers of the
army, that they were in many places assailable in the
forenoon, and that by the continuance of the same
fire for a few hours longer, they would be in such a
state as to render it desperate, with our numbers, to
attempt to maintain them.  We at that time could
not fire a single gun; only one 8-inch and little more
than 100 Cohorn shells remained.  A diversion by
the French ships of war that lay in the mouth of York
River was to be expected.

Our numbers had been diminished by the enemy's
fire, but particularly by sickness, and the strength and
spirits of those in the works were much exhausted,
by the fatigue of constant watching and unremitting
duty.  Under all these circumstances, I thought it
would have been wanton and inhuman to the last
degree to sacrifice the lives of this small body of gal-

lant soldiers, who had ever behaved with so much fidelity and courage, by exposing them to an assault which, from the numbers and precautions of the enemy, could not fail to succeed. I therefore proposed to capitulate; and I have the honor to enclose to your Excellency the copy of the correspondence between General Washington and me on that subject, and the terms of capitulation agreed upon. I sincerely lament that better could not be obtained, but I have neglected nothing in my power to alleviate the misfortune and distress of both officers and soldiers. The men are well clothed and provided with necessaries, and I trust will be regularly supplied by the means of the officers that are permitted to remain with them.

The treatment, in general, that we have received from the enemy since our surrender has been perfectly good and proper, but the kindness and attention that has been shown to us by the French officers in particular—their delicate sensibility of our situation —their generous and pressing offer of money, both public and private, to any amount—has really gone beyond what I can possibly describe, and will, I hope, make an impression on the breast of every British officer, whenever the fortune of war should put any of them into our power.

# WASHINGTON REPORTS THE YORKTOWN
# SURRENDER

*THIS report to Congress of the surrender of Cornwallis was written by Washington in the Moore house near Yorktown, Va., October 19, 1781, where the terms of surrender had been dictated earlier in the day. Curiously enough, General Benjamin Lincoln, who the year before had surrendered Charleston, S. C., to Cornwallis, was chosen by Washington to receive Cornwallis's sword at Yorktown. The terms at Yorktown were the same as those at Charleston.*

*Cornwallis, whom ill health confined to his headquarters in Yorktown, was represented on the momentous occasion by General O'Hara, of his staff. The courtesy and generosity of the victorious allies have been warmly attested by the British commander, who was tendered an elaborate dinner by General Washington, at which all the staff officers of the French, British and American military and naval forces were present.*

I HAVE the honor to inform Congress that a reduction of the British army, under the command of Lord Cornwallis, is most happily effected. The unremitted ardor, which actuated every officer and soldier in the combined army on this occasion, has principally led to this important event at an earlier period than my most sanguine hopes had induced me to expect.

The singular spirit of emulation, which animated the whole army from the first commencement of our operations, has filled my mind with the highest pleasure and satisfaction, and had given me the happiest presages of success.

On the 17th instant, a letter was received from Lord Cornwallis, proposing a meeting of commis-

sioners to consult on terms for the surrender of the
posts of York and Gloucester. This letter (the first
which had passed between us) opened a correspondence, a copy of which I do myself the honor to enclose; that correspondence was followed by the defini-
tive capitulation, which was agreed to and signed on
the 19th, a copy of which is also herewith transmitted
and which, I hope, will meet the approbation of
Congress.

I should be wanting in the feelings of gratitude,
did I not mention on this occasion, with the warmest
sense of acknowledgment, the very cheerful and able
assistance which I have received in the course of our
operation from his Excellency the Count de Rochambeau and all his officers of every rank in their respective capacities. Nothing could equal the zeal of our
allies, but the emulating spirit of the American officers, whose ardor would not suffer their exertions to
be exceeded.

The very uncommon degree of duty and fatigue,
which the nature of the service required from the
officers and engineers and artillery of both armies,
obliges me particularly to mention the obligations I
am under to the commanding and other officers of
those corps.

I wish it was in my power to express to Congress
how much I feel myself indebted to the Count de
Grasse and the officers of the fleet under his command, for the distinguished aid and support which
has been afforded by them, between whom and the

army the most happy concurrence of sentiments and views has subsisted, and from whom every possible coöperation has been experienced, which the most harmonious intercourse could afford.

# WASHINGTON RESIGNS HIS COMMISSION
## TO CONGRESS

*By Rev. William Gordon, D.D.*

*D*R. *GORDON was an English minister, who came to America in 1770 and occupied a pulpit at Roxbury, Mass., until 1786, when he returned to England. During the Revolutionary War he sided with the colonists, making careful researches while the war was in progress, and in 1788 published his "History of the Rise and Independence of the United States, Including the Late War," from which this account is derived. It has been considered one of the most valuable sources for the history of the Revolution.*

*It is probable that during the year preceding the resignation of his commission to Congress on December 23, 1783, Washington, had he so desired, could have founded a monarchy, sustained by his army. He took the course, on the contrary, of quelling this disposition on the part of his soldiers whenever it showed itself.*

*G*ENERAL WASHINGTON, after delivering in his accounts, hastened to Annapolis, where he arrived on the evening of the 19th of December. The next day he informed Congress of his arrival in that city, with the intention of asking leave to resign the commission he had the honor of holding in their service, and desired to know their pleasure in what manner it would be most proper to offer his resignation—whether in writing or at an audience. They resolved that it should be at a public audience, the following Tuesday at twelve o'clock. The general had been so reserved with regard to the time of his intended resignation, that Congress had not the least apprehension of its being either so soon or so sudden.

When the day was arrived, and the hour approached for fixing the patriotic character of the American Chief, the gallery was filled with a beautiful group of elegant ladies, and some graced the floor of Congress. On this were likewise the governor, council and legislature of Maryland, several general officers, the consul general of France, and the respectable citizens of Annapolis. Congress were seated and covered, as representatives of the sovereignty of the Union, the spectators were uncovered and standing. The general was introduced to a chair by the secretary, who, after a decent interval, ordered silence. A short pause ensued, when the Honorable Thomas Mifflin, the president, informed the general, that "the United States in Congress assembled were prepared to receive his communications": on which he rose with great dignity, and delivered this address:

"Mr. President, The great events on which my resignation depended having at length taken place, I have now the honor of offering my sincere congratulations to Congress, and of presenting myself before them to surrender into their hands the trust committed to me, and to claim the indulgence of retiring from the service of my country.

"Happy in the confirmation of our independence and sovereignty, and pleased with the opportunity afforded the United States, of becoming a respectable nation, I resign with satisfaction the appointment I accepted with diffidence—a diffidence in my abilities to accomplish so arduous a task; which however was superseded by a confidence in the rectitude of our cause, the support of the supreme power of the Union, and the patronage of Heaven.

"The successful termination of the war has verified the most sanguine expectations; and my gratitude for the interposition of providence, and the assistance I have received from my countrymen, increases with every review of the momentous contest.

"While I repeat my obligations to the army in general, I should do injustice to my own feelings not to acknowledge, in this place, the peculiar services and distinguished merits of the gentlemen who have been attached to my person during the war. It was impossible the choice of confidential officers to compose my family should have been more fortunate. Permit me, sir, to recommend in particular, those who have continued in the service to the present moment, as worthy of the favorable notice and patronage of Congress.

"I consider it as an indispensable duty to close this last act of my official life by commending the interests of our dearest country to the protection of Almighty God, and those who have the superintendence of them to His holy keeping.

"Having now finished the work assigned me, I retire from the great theater of action, and bidding an affectionate farewell to this august body, under whose orders I have so long acted, I here offer my commission, and take my leave of all the employments of public life."

The general was so powerfully impressed, with the great and interesting scenes that crowded in upon his imagination while speaking, that he would have been scarce able to have uttered more than the closing period. He advanced and delivered to the President his commission, with a copy of his address. Having resumed his place, he received in a standing posture the . . . answer of Congress; which the President delivered with elegance; but not without such a sensibility as changed, and spread a degree of paleness over, his countenance. . . .

# WASHINGTON BIDS HIS ARMY FAREWELL

*THE scene which attended Washington's farewell to the rank and file of his army at Rocky Hill, near Princeton, New Jersey, on Sunday, November 2 1783, was only less affecting than his formal leave-taking with his leading officers at Fraunce's Tavern in New York a month later when Washington said: "With a heart full of love and gratitude I must now take my leave of you. I most devoutly wish that your latter days may be as prosperous and happy as your former ones have been glorious and honorable. . . . I shall be obliged to you if each will come and take me by the hand." Many of the officers, including Washington, wept audibly.*

*His much more elaborate address at Princeton, written in the third person, is said to have been prepared by Alexander Hamilton. In tone it is very similar to Washington's splendid letter of June 8, 1783, to the Governors of the States with regard to the necessity of establishing a firm and dignified Federal Government.*

THE United States in Congress assembled, after giving the most honorable testimony to the Federal armies, and presenting them with the thanks of their country for their long, eminent and faithful services, having thought proper, by their proclamation bearing date the 18th day of October last, to discharge such part of the troops as were engaged for the war, and to permit the officers on furlough to retire from services from and after to-morrow; which proclamation having been communicated in the public papers for the information and government of all concerned, it only remains for the Commander-in-Chief to address himself once more, and that for the last time, to the armies of the United States (however widely dispersed the in-

dividuals who compose them may be), and to bid
them an affectionate, a long farewell.

But before the Commander-in-Chief takes final
leave of those he holds most dear, he wishes to indulge
himself a few moments in calling to mind a slight
review of the past. He will then take the liberty of
exploring with his military friends their future prospects, of advising the general line of conduct, which,
in his opinion, ought to be pursued; and he will conclude the address by expressing the obligations he feels
himself under for the spirited and able assistance he
has experienced from them, in the performance of
an arduous office.

A contemplation of the complete attainment (at a
period earlier than could have been expected) of the
object, for which we contended against so formidable
a power, cannot but inspire us with astonishment and
gratitude. The disadvantageous circumstances on
our part, under which the war was undertaken, can
never be forgotten. The singular interpositions of
Providence in our feeble condition were such, as could
scarcely escape the attention of the most unobserving;
while the unparalleled perseverance of the armies of
the United States, through almost every possible suffering and discouragement for the space of eight long
years, was little short of a standing miracle.

It is not the meaning nor within the compass of this
address, to detail the hardship peculiarly incident to
our service, or to describe the distresses, which in
several instances have resulted from the extremes of

hunger and nakedness, combined with the rigors of an inclement season; nor is it necessary to dwell on the dark side of our past affairs. Every American officer and soldier must now console himself for any unpleasant circumstances, which may have occurred, by a recollection of the uncommon scenes in which he has been called to act no inglorious part, and the astonishing events of which he has been a witness; events which have seldom, if ever before, taken place on the stage of human action; nor can they probably ever happen again. For who has before seen a disciplined army formed at once from such raw materials? Who, that was not a witness, could imagine that the most violent local prejudices would cease so soon; and that men, who came from the different parts of the continent, strongly disposed by the habits of education to despise and quarrel with each other, would instantly become but one patriotic band of brothers? Or who, that was not on the spot, can trace the steps by which such a wonderful revolution has been effected, and such a glorious period put to all our warlike toils?

It is universally acknowledged that the enlarged prospects of happiness, opened by the confirmation of our independence and sovereignty, almost exceeds the power of description. And shall not the brave men, who have contributed so essentially to these inestimable acquisitions, retiring victorious from the field of war to the field of agriculture, participate in all the blessings, which have been obtained? In such a republic, who will exclude them from the rights of citizens, and the fruits of their labors? In such a country, so happily circumstanced, the pursuits of commerce and the cultivation of the soil will unfold to industry the certain road to competence. To those hardy soldiers, who are actuated by the spirit of adventure, the fisheries will afford ample and profitable employment; and the extensive and fertile regions of the West will yield a most happy asylum to those, who, fond of domestic enjoyment, are seeking for personal independence. Nor is it possible to conceive that any one of the United States will prefer a national bankruptcy, and a dissolution of the Union, to a compliance with the requisition of Congress, and the payment of its just debts; so that the officers and soldiers may expect considerable assistance, in recomencing their civil occupations, from the public, which must and will most inevitably be paid.

In order to effect this desirable purpose, and to remove the prejudices, which may have taken possession of the minds of any of the good people of the States, it is earnestly recommended to all the troops, that, with strong attachments of the Union, they should carry with them into civil society the most conciliating dispositions, and that they should prove themselves not less virtuous and useful as citizens than they have been persevering and victorious as soldiers. What though there should be some envious individuals who are unwilling to pay the debt the public has contracted, or to yield the tribute due to merit; yet let such unworthy treatment produce no invective, or any instance of intemperate conduct. Let it be remembered that the unbiased voice of the free citizens of the United States has promised the just reward and given the merited applause. Let it be known and remembered that the reputation of the Federal armies is established beyond the reach of malevolence; and let a consciousness of their achievements and fame still incite the men who composed them to honorable actions; under the persuasion that the private virtues of economy, prudence and industry, will not be less amiable in civil life, than more splendid qualities of valor, perseverance, and enterprise were in the field. Every one may rest assured that much, very much, of the future happiness of the officers and men, will depend upon the wise and manly conduct which shall be adopted by them when they are mingled with the great body of the community. And, although the General has so frequently given it as his opinion in the most public and explicit manner, that, unless the principles of the Federal government were properly supported, and the powers of the Union increased, the honor, diginity, and justice of the nation would be lost forever; yet he cannot help repeating, on this occasion, so interesting a sentiment, and leaving it as his last injunction to every officer and soldier, who may view the subject in the same serious point of light, to add his best endeavors to those of his worthy fellow citizens towards effecting these great and valuable purposes, on which our very existence as a nation so materially depends.

The Commander-in-Chief conceives little is now wanting to enable the soldier to change the military character into that of the citizen, but that steady and decent tenor of behavior which has generally distinguished, not only the army under his immediate command, but the different detachments and separate armies, through the course of the war. From their good sense and prudence he anticipates the happiest consequences; and, while he congratulates them on the glorious occasion which renders their services in the field no longer necessary, he wishes to express the strong obligations he feels himself under for the assistance he has received from every class and in every instance. He presents his thanks in the most serious and affectionate manner to the general officers, as well for their counsel, on many interesting occasions, as for their ardor in promoting the success of the plans he had adopted; to the commandants of regiments and corps, and to the other officers for their great zeal and attention in carrying his orders promptly into execution; to the staff for their alacrity and exactness in performing the duties of their several departments; and to the non-commissioned officers and private soldiers for their extraordinary patience and suffering, as well as their invincible fortitude in action. To the various branches of the army, the general takes this last and solemn opportunity of professing his inviolable attachment and friendship. He wishes more than bare professions were in his power; that he were really able to be useful to them all in future life. He flatters himself, however, they will do him the justice to believe, that whatever could with propriety be attempted by him has been done.

And being now to conclude these his last public orders, to take his ultimate leave in a short time of the military character, and to bid a final adieu to the armies he has so long had the honor to command, he can only again offer in their behalf his recommendations to their grateful country, and his prayers to the God of armies. May ample justice be done them here, and may the choicest of Heaven's favors, both here and hereafter, attend those, who, under the Divine auspices, have secured innumerable blessings for others. With these wishes and this benediction, the Commander-in-Chief is about to retire from service. The curtain of separation will soon be drawn, and the military scene to him will be closed forever.